For Rosalie

Kinoetics: *Signs of Conflict* Our Personal Body Language

Kinoetics Publishing
www.kinoetics.com / (877) 726-2290

Library of Congress Card Number 00-190737
ISBN 0-9700739-0-9
Printed in Canada.

Photographs by Concha Navarro
Illustrations by David Wheelock, Melanie Dahl, Chris Bergerson

Grateful acknowledgement is made for permission to reprint previously published material:

The Alphabet Versus the Goddess by Leonard Shlain, copyright © 1998 by Leonard Shlain. Used by permission of Viking Penguin, a division of Penguin Putnam, Inc.

Brain and Conscious Experience, Robert Sperry, ed. J. Eccles, © 1966, Springer-Verlag GmbH & Co., KG.

Dragon Rises, Red Bird Flies: Psychology and Chinese Medicine, Leon Hammer, © 1991, Station Hill Press.

Hand and Mind: What Gestures Reveal About Thought, David McNeill, © 1992, University of Chicago Press.

Extract from *Manwatching* by Desmond Morris published by Jonathan Cape. Used by permission of The Random House Group Limited.

Excerpt from *Nonverbal Communication in Human Interaction,* Mark L. Knapp, © 1972 by Holt, Rinehart and Winston, printed by permission of the publisher.

From *Reading Faces,* by Bellak & Baker, © 1980. Reprinted by permission of Henry Holt & Co., LLC.

Excerpt from *The Right Mind: Making Sense of the Hemispheres,* copyright © 1997 by Robert E. Ornstein, reprinted by permission of Harcourt, Inc.

Telling Lies, by Paul Ekman, copyright © 1985, W.W. Norton.

Kinoetics
Signs of Conflict

Our Personal
Body Language

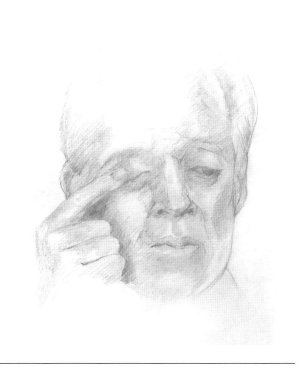

by William Linson, M.D.

In Appreciation:

Rosalie Deliso Newsome, Ph.D., who, as a friend and associate, first encouraged me to begin recording these observations so many years ago.

Marcia Hart, M.A., who introduced me to kinesiology and
Danial Whiteside and Gordon Stokes, pioneers in psychoemotional kinesiology (One Brain), as well as to the work of Goodheart, Thie, and Diamond, among others, over 20 years ago. Marcia was also helpful in clarifying symbolism in the illustrations.

Dietrich Klinghardt, M.D., for the opportunity to observe his work and for recommending Scott Walker, D.C., who helped me pull these many concepts together (NET seminars).

Paul Ekman, Ph.D., for meaningful references and reprints of his work.

For help in finally putting all this material together:
Melanie Dahl, who has assisted me over the last ten years. In addition to typing and collating this work, she offered ideas, edited, found most of the quotes, provided illustrations of the brain and the cover design concept. (That's her evaluating from the "K" on the cover.)

My son Bruce for the principal editing job, which was so helpful. ("Don't take it personally, Pop.") My sister Dossie for persistent encouragement. ("Come on, what are you waiting for?") My daughter Erica for her inspiration.

Dave Wheelock, whose computer and graphic skills, patience and good humor, were of immeasurable help.

Good friends who read and commented, especially Bob Hawley, Linnea Polichetti, Herb Weissman, Dan Peterson, Kate Wright, and Sandy Hyde.

Tom Pritscher for encouragement and the term *Kinoetics*.

Kinoetics

Signs of Conflict: Our Personal Body Language

Contents

The body doesn't lie.

- John Diamond

Introduction

What if we had a way to get to the deeper levels of our being? We do. It is through our own bodies. The language of the body, spoken through movement, can aid in identifying unconscious determinants of behavior. Body language may also signal the emotions that provoke or accompany behavior, and sometimes even indicate the motivation behind it. Most studies of body language have focused on facial expression and gestures, but many other signals that are also transmitted nonverbally have not received the same kind of attention. (See Chapter 2, "Body Language: *A Brief Overview.*")

Where the heart lies, let the brain lie also.

- Robert Browning

This book explores the significance of a relatively overlooked aspect of body language, that is, the frequent, brief self-touching motions and other self-referential actions, such as lip biting, that occur in response to internal cues. These movements are clear indicators of the state of a person's mind and seem to reflect the efforts of the unconscious mind to bring the person into balance—not only to physical homeostasis but to mental and emotional balance as well.

The premise of this work is that **conflict** *typically has an associated physical response, and is often accompanied by self-referential touching of one's body, which symbolically manifests what one is thinking and feeling.* While the physical response *may* be perceived consciously, it is often barely perceptible to the conscious mind. Just as frequently, the individual is unaware of any sensation that has caused him to bring the hand to the body, head, or limbs, or show other signs of this *personal body language*.

While the impetus to these movements seems to be the body's effort to regulate energy distribution and flow, the benefit of the concomitant symbolism is that we can decipher the associated hidden meanings.

Kinoetics is the designation I have chosen for the specific body movements that reflect unconscious mental activity (Greek *kin*, to move; set in motion + *noetics*, cognition; of the mind; the act of knowing).

The self-referential touching that will be described has a very different significance than gestures. Gestures constitute an external or social dialogue, whereas the motions of Kinoetics reflect what is going on within oneself, an internal personal dialogue. That is, Kinoetics constitutes a personal body language and is not intended for communication with others.

While the overall impression (gestalt) of such a motion is perceptible to other individuals, they usually do not consciously understand—but may well intuit—that the motion has significance. Curiously, even though a self-referential touch concerns highly personal material, the individual manifesting a Kinoetic response is most often also unaware of the significance of the movement—that it has meaning. To gain an understanding of the meaning of one's own body language, a heightened conscious attention—awareness of what one is feeling and doing—is required. An introduction to this process is the purpose of this book.

*Go to your bosom,
Knock there,
and ask your heart
what it doth know.*

- Shakespeare

*Life happens at
the level of events
not words.
Trust movement.*

\- Alfred Adler

Section I

The Forces that Move Us

Chapter 1

Expressions of the Unconscious

Over the years, my work as a psychiatrist has given me the best possible opportunity to observe the significance and symbolism of the unspoken language communicated by the body, so-called body language. This nonverbal communication, "spoken" through facial expression and body motion and posture, often conveys more than the spoken word and is more honest than the spoken word. In fact, unless done consciously with the intention of deceiving others, body language is highly accurate and specific.

O shame! Where is thy blush?

- Shakespeare

My initial interest in this area began to develop in medical school with an introduction to the numerous studies showing the exquisite responsiveness of nervous system physiology to emotion. The knowledge that, for example, the lining of the stomach could "blush" or conversely could show pallor, similar to color changes in the face in response to emotion, gave me the awareness of *how profoundly important all observable body changes are as clues to our mental state.* These changes occur automatically in response to processes largely outside of our awareness, i.e., in our subconscious mind.

The "discovery" of the unconscious mind did not occur with Sigmund Freud, as is popularly thought—postulations as to its existence and function can be traced throughout history. Plato, in the *Meno*, wrote of Socrates eliciting from an uneducated boy an "unconscious knowledge" of a mathematical theorem; he also makes reference to the unconscious in *The Republic*. In the 1700s, the importance of the unconscious was specifically addressed by philosophers and writers Jean Jacques Rousseau and Johann von Herder. In 1846, the German physician Carl

Gustav Carus wrote *Psyche: On the Development of the Soul*, in which he noted, "The key to an understanding of the nature of the conscious life of the soul lies in the sphere of the unconscious" (1851, p. 1). Years later Freud became familiar with this work.

In the introduction to Carus's book, psychologist James Hillman writes, "Psychological ideas have long histories....That the mind has a *dark field* (Liebnitz and Kant) or has access to a *storehouse of imaginal memory* (Augustine) over and against the light of consciousness is a long-standing metaphor....But it took the nineteenth century to formulate these archtypal fantasies into a theory of the unconscious" (p. vii).

Indeed, it was not until 1895 that Freud first published case studies on the treatment of hysteria from which he derived hypotheses about the unconscious mind, and which remain at the core of psychoanalytic theory. Freud, better than anyone previously, began to understand the *system* of the unconscious mind, that is, how it operated as the hidden force motivating and orchestrating so much of human behavior, moods, and even physical illness. In doing so, he created a new paradigm, a model with which to understand human behavior. Whatever defects were present in Freud's system, particularly a certain aversion to looking at issues we now refer to under the heading of spirituality, he nonetheless provided the opportunity for a revolution in psychology equivalent to that created by Darwin in the fields of biology and anthropology.

Although known as a disciple of Freud's, C.G. Jung was internationally known in the world of psychology before his relationship with Freud began in 1907, a friendship that ended abruptly just five short years later due to Jung's insistence on a larger concept of mind.

It is our less conscious thoughts and our less conscious actions which mainly mould our lives and the lives of those who spring from us.

- Samuel Butler

Jung, however:

> *borrowed from Freud the conception of conscious and unconscious spheres, of a mind mediated by a defended ego, a source of psychic energy called the libido, and a mission to reclaim territory from the unconscious. Beyond these similarities, their differences were profound; while Freud's model tended to be mechanistic, analytic and reductive to basic causes, Jung's was more organic, expansive, and unfolding to purposive ends* (Hampden-Turner, 1981, p. 44).

Jung's view of the unconscious evolved from that of the personal unconscious of repressed emotions and memories to the notion of a collective unconscious, wherein lie emotions and visions that come from some psychic depth related to all human experience, even from pre-hominid history.

Without the groundbreaking work of these men of genius and the brilliant contributions made by others to our understanding of depth psychology, we would still be in the dark about the dynamic forces that shape our lives. However, our efforts at psychotherapeutic intervention lag far behind the theoretical framework given us by these great pioneers. We still lack tools to provide immediate, beneficial, and transformative feedback about the thought/feeling complex, disturbances of which are so clearly contributory to illness. Furthermore, as long-term depth therapy is clearly a luxury that most people cannot afford (and even then sometimes fails to produce the intended results), it is imperative that we develop more effective techniques or tools to help individuals effectively access unconscious material and achieve wholeness through an integration of both the conscious and unconscious minds.

The unconscious psyche is not only immensely old, it is also capable of growing into an equally remote future.

- Carl Jung

While depth psychologists have long held to the notion that the language of the unconscious manifests most obviously in dreams, and to a much lesser extent as inadvertent revelation (e.g., slips of the tongue), we have come to realize the benefit of knowing that the body always responds to the unconscious in some manner. It was an awareness of this concept that led Diogenes so long ago to comment on the relationship between blushing and innocence.

The challenging process of adventuring into the unconscious as approached by Freud and Jung was through the verbal production of their subjects; descriptions of body expression/language were not included in their clinical studies. As part of his analytic technique, Freud placed his patients on the couch where bodily motion was minimal and facial expression difficult to observe, particularly as Freud sat behind the patient. Many analysts used the same method, although some, including Jung and his followers, began to see patients face to face.

Although some of the professionals who began to study the significance of body language (which received increasing attention in the 1960s and 1970s) were psychiatrists, training in that field remains notoriously deficient in calling attention to nonverbal communication and its importance. In my own training, for example, there was virtually no reference to this topic. Today, body language is studied principally by psychologists and social anthropologists. Yet it does not seem to have impacted clinical training in psychology to a significant degree either. Not surprisingly, those health professionals who have a high regard for the body as an integral part of *mind*, e.g., many body workers, naturopaths, chiropractors, and kinesiologists, often have a greater interest in this topic as they are trained to understand the body comprehensively, including its role as a communication medium.

(Diogenes) saw a youth blushing, and addressed him, "Courage, my boy! that is the complexion of virtue."

The numerous and extensive studies of body language have primarily focused on interactive communication between individuals, particularly facial expression and gestures in humans and animals, as well as the context in which they occur, both behavioral and social.[1] Facial expression is the most evident body language, as the face is the principal communicator of our emotional state. Individuals may express, purposefully or not, a pure (single) emotion, mixed emotions, or may modify or even feign the emotional response. Gestures with the hands convey a body language that is intentionally directed toward others and communicate with varying degrees of specificity; thus they constitute an interpersonal (social) language. (President Clinton gestures in the photograph on page 6.)

In solitude,
where we are
least alone.

- Lord Byron

This work, however, calls attention to the spontaneous, relatively discreet, usually brief body motions that occur in response to cues from one's inner self. These actions constitute a personal body language, a private communication that is manifested in most instances by touching oneself, primarily with the hand, although other parts of the body may be used such as the teeth biting the lower lip. Head and foot movements may also serve the same purpose. These particular body actions are *intra*personal (within oneself), occurring as a person responds to internal cues that are triggered by thoughts, memories, and emotions, and reflect *inner conflict*—often referred to as intrapsychic conflict. Another way to put it is that most aspects of self-touching are a form of personal dialogue, "part of me" communicating with another "part of me" when experiencing internal conflict. (Note the hand position

---

[1] Behavioral context includes territorial, protective, and feeding behaviors; social context refers to the attitudes and moods relating to social interaction including courtship, deception, rank in the social hierarchy, etc.

President Clinton gestures to the press about the Lewinsky matter.

Vice President Gore indicates conflict about belief. (See the section on Head.)

(AP/Wide World Photos)

of Vice President Al Gore—and his facial expression—in the same photo facing page.) While gestures comprise a nonverbal language that appears to be understood by everyone in that culture, *our personal body language is most often not consciously understood even by the one who is "speaking."* And while gestures occur almost exclusively in a social setting, our personal body responses are as likely to occur when we are alone as when we are in the presence of others.

These intrapersonal body responses differ from gestures in that the movements are not only primarily involuntary, but they are also usually unconscious and *not intended for communication to others.* While these movements may appear random, they have a purpose arising from the unconscious. An understanding of personal body language can provide valuable information on elements about a person's unconscious mental and emotional activity.

With affection beaming in one eye, and calculation shining out of the other.

- Charles Dickens

The internal conflict that prompts these body responses is often the result of the *two different points of view of the two hemispheres of the brain.* Each hemisphere provides a different angle of viewing, so to speak, analogous to the two different angles of viewing that the eyes provide to give us binocular vision.

As each eye can operate without the simultaneous functioning of the other, so can each hemisphere of the brain, for each hemisphere has its own sphere of consciousness. Thus, when a person says "on the one hand" and presents a point of view, and then indicates a differing or even oppositional point of view "on the other hand," we see a manifestation of the position of the two hemispheres in respect to the matter being considered. Because each hemisphere serves the opposite side of the body, the right side and hand represent the view of the left brain, and the left side and hand represent the view of the right brain. These disparate views and operating modes are equally important. If they can be experienced and integrated simultaneously, we have "whole brain" thinking. Ideally, the integration of these opposite sides of our brain provides us with a multi-dimensional view, allowing for the fullness and richness of experience. However, these perspectives can be, and often are, so opposite that an internal struggle ensues, which is evidenced by motions of personal body language.

If the disparity between these points of view is sufficiently great, a gross imbalance develops between the brain hemispheres. At this point, the person will be prompted internally (and unconsciously) to attempt to resolve this discomforting imbalance. The most effective motion in the effort to aid hemispheric integration is that of bringing a hand to the forehead, as can be seen in the photographs of former Secretary of State Madeleine Albright and retired quarterback Dan Marino on pages 10 and 11. The situations confronting these two individuals were extreme; lesser degrees of imbalance are often accompanied by a less dramatic positioning of the hand to the forehead, such as if one were covering the eyes to focus one's view.

Remember when life's path is steep to keep your mind even.

- Horace

An interesting historical note that is pertinent to this material is the significance of one of Freud's early, and overlooked, observations documented in the book *Psychological Conflict and Defense* (Mahl, 1971, pp. 8-11). In October, 1885, Freud traveled to Paris to study under the great neurologist Charcot, whose pioneering work in hysteria helped Freud formulate his ideas about the unconscious mind. While in France, he also visited Hippolyte Bernheim, a prominent professor of medicine, and watched him work with a patient who was experiencing difficulty remembering certain suggestions made to her while she had been under hypnosis. Freud wrote that Bernheim "laid his hand on her forehead to help her recall them. And lo and behold! She ended up describing everything…." Later, working with his famous patient Lucy R., Freud experienced a similar difficulty and, remembering Bernheim's action, he "pressed her head" with his hand, and Lucy R. did, in fact, remember some of her repressed memories and emotions. Although this "hands on" approach to accessing unconscious material appeared to be highly effective, for various reasons it did not become a significant component in Freud's psychoanalytic process nor in that of his successors.

With my hand upon his head Is my benediction said.

- Elizabeth Barrett
  Browning

The importance of the action of placing a hand on the head, in a religious blessing for example, has been universally understood at the intuitive level. Empirical reason indicates that the energy within the hand, when placed upon the forehead, facilitates the cooperation between the two brains, bridging the gap between them in the same way the internal bridge (the corpus callosum) allows the two hemispheres to communicate and transmit information. Interestingly, not only does the corpus callosum consist of the nerve fibers that allow the two brain hemispheres to correspond, but *it also has the ability to block communication between them* through inhibitory pathways. Today, there is awareness of the utility and implication of touching the forehead to aid hemispheric integration among a wide range of health professionals, particularly kinesiologists and chiropractors.

The aspect of self-referential touching to which I am referring is related to this imbalance between our brain hemispheres (caused by or resulting in a sense of conflict) and has not, to the best of my knowledge, been presented from the perspective I offer here. The spontaneous and quite specific body motions explored in this book are characterized by their frequency and relatively short duration. It comes closest to a few types

The photos on these two pages show one of the most important and useful Kinoetic responses—the hand to the forehead.

Overwhelming stimuli—traumatic thoughts, memories, or feelings—cause this spontaneous response to conflict in an attempt to regain internal hemispheric balance.

The great quarterback Dan Marino reacts after a big loss in an important playoff game. He retired soon after.

(AP/Wide World Photos)

Former Secretary of State Madeleine Albright confers with top brass and aides about Bosnia, a conflict that seemed to have no resolution.

(AP/Wide World Photos)

of self-touching that have been defined and labeled by previous investigators and authors, and these categories will be discussed in Chapter 2, "Body Language: *A Brief Overview.*"

This work is the result of my observations of self-touching and other body motion, primarily in the therapeutic setting, as well as the associated expressed or implied emotion occurring in conjunction with the subject matter under discussion.[2] I have been encouraged by the usefulness of the interpretive symbolism of personal body language, as *the process markedly facilitates psychotherapy*. It was this noticeable efficacy in therapy early in my work that prompted me to pursue this line of inquiry.

Observing the readiness with which individuals in therapy learn to recognize the cues and symbolism of self-referential touching and become aware of the significance of the motions, I realized also the potential usefulness of understanding personal body language to anyone looking for assistance on the road to conflict resolution and personal growth.

This work has not been validated in structured studies by other researchers, but, if it is found to be useful, I hope this information will enhance and expand the study of self-referential touching. To this end, I welcome observations made by others.

Often the wisdom of the body clarifies the despair of the spirit.

- Marion Woodman

---

[2] The descriptions of the inherent symbolism of the motions were supported by unconscious signaling while a person was in a mild trance. The unconscious readily signaled meaning, and the interpretation of the meaning could then be used consciously by that individual.

Chapter 2

Body Language: *A Brief Overview*

Observing a person in therapy, the most reliable indicators or clues that point to the truth that individual is seeking, grouped under the heading of *body language* or *nonverbal communication*, are facial expression, qualities of the eyes,[1] qualities of the voice including voice tone,[2] body posture and position, and body motion.

We perceive all these signals at once, of course, and collectively they create an overall impression. Yet, if we would increase our understanding of human behavior, we must break out individual components for study, all the while recognizing that an undue emphasis on any one part will distort our view of the whole (gestalt).

An early leader in the field of nonverbal communication, R.L. Birdwhistell, researched and wrote about what he termed *kinesics* as early as 1952. He pointed out the difficulty of analyzing the meaning of body movement as communication, noting that the probable amounts of

---

[1] Eye quality includes contact and aversion, which in turn includes the direction in which the eyes are averted, as well as moisture ("misty-eyed"), focused or unfocused ("blank" expression), and pupillary dilatation. Moisture suggests sadness, but the action of the muscles surrounding the eyes completes the expression of sadness.

[2] The various schools of psychotherapy have concentrated most attention on *what* is said, i.e., the content, but another major aspect of nonverbal communication is *how* something is said. Such things as one's voice quality and tone of voice are particularly important. It has been said that 90% of problems in communication are due to tone of voice. One can also refer to the intensity and pitch of voice as well as other characteristics.

information generated by a body per second, given off as "minimally discernible changes in sound, light, and odor stream," were relatively enormous. Thus, he called attention to the possibility of being swamped with the flood of data from the body. Undaunted, however, he went on to attempt to break down and analyze this data. Simply put, he identified all components of body movement from the smallest to the largest, with all gradations in between, and used them as building blocks or units to construct a language, which he then transcribed. With this approach, he found kinesics to be analogous to linguistics (1970).

Mark Knapp, author of one of the first comprehensive reference texts on nonverbal behavior (and to which I refer any reader interested in this topic, especially for its extensive bibiography), wrote:

> *Nonverbal communication should not be studied as an isolated unit, but as an inseparable part of the total communication process. Nonverbal communication may serve to repeat, contradict, substitute, complement, accent, or regulate verbal communication. Nonverbal communication is important because of the role it plays in the total communication system, the tremendous quantity of informational cues it gives in any particular situation, and because of its use in fundamental areas of our daily life. Nonverbal behavior is partly taught, partly imitative, and partly instinctive* (1972, p. 21).

Gestures and other body language, as well as the personal body language that is the subject in this work, are observed, of course, not only in the therapeutic setting but occur with great frequency in everyone in all environments. Perhaps because they are so readily and easily observed, the areas of nonverbal behavior that have been studied extensively are facial expression and gestures.[3] I include here a brief look at those topics and also include references and ideas related to the limited research on self-touching.

Facial Expression

Since the face is the most expressive part of the body by far, it is only natural that this is where the attention of researchers has been focused for many years. Scholarly and clinical works continue to be published on this topic, although they are usually little read by the general public. On the mass market, however, "how to" materials on reading faces are routinely popular.

It is not generally well known that one of Charles Darwin's three monumental works was on the topic of facial expression. His book, *The Expression of the Emotions in Man and Animals*, was published in 1872 after *The Origin of Species* and *The Descent of Man*. More than anyone before him, Darwin accumulated evidence that facial expression is largely innate and similar around the world.

Paul Ekman[4] and his colleagues are credited with confirming the work of Darwin, not only in literate Eastern and Western cultures, but also in contemporary preliterate cultures, especially in New Guinea. They noted

---

[3] Other areas of body language influencing communication include physical characteristics, from different skin colors, height and weight, to breath and body odor. Research has also been done on the way in which humans use both their personal and social space (proxemics), the effect of personal adornments, and the environments in which individuals interact.

[4] Paul Ekman has been a leading researcher in the study of facial expression and other nonverbal communication for decades. His extensive writing includes the introduction to a third edition of Darwin's *Expression of the Emotions*. Ekman's work on facial expression remains at the forefront of continuing research and is currently being used at the Salk Center in La Jolla to assist in the design of a computer system that will identify emotions in individuals. He is Professor of Psychology and Director of the Human Interaction laboratory at the University of California, San Francisco.

that facial expression varied due to cultural influences that modified this innate response. Thus, facial expressions are better understood within the same culture and, as we experience in our personal lives, they are understood better yet by people who know each other well.

Facial expressions or configurations indicate one's mood or affect, and may be in agreement with what is being said, contradict it, or have no apparent relationship. We are all familiar with the idea that the look on a person's face may betray his feelings to others while the individual himself may be unaware of the emotion being expressed.

Gestures

Originally, the word *gesture* referred to a form of manual communication the study of which can be traced back to Cicero (106-43 B.C.) and Quintilian (ca. 35-95 A.D.) whose interest in the topic focused on the use of gestures in oratory. It wasn't until the 17th century that gestures gained attention as a field of study. John Bulwer (*Chirologia* and *Chironomia*, 1644) began to look at gestures as a speech surrogate and ultimately recognized the possibility of developing a manual language for the deaf.

It has been proposed that gestures comprised the evolutionary origins of language; there is good reason to believe that early hominids used a form of communication that was predominantly gestural. The shift to vocal language occurred when the brain and the appropriate vocal apparatus developed. We began talking to each other, first in a protolanguage, then with increasingly more sophisticated elements, leading to a fully constituted language (Harre & Lamb, 1983, p. 254-255).

Gestures include any movement of the body, head, arms, hands, or face that is *expressive* of an idea, opinion, or emotion, such as the gestures of an orator or gestures of anger or fear—they are *imagistic*. Thus, gestures comprise a body language that is directed toward others and is, consciously or not, communication to them. Gestures may be variably categorized and many are similar throughout the world, but many differ radically from one culture to another.

One of the earliest investigators, Edward Sapir, noted in 1927, "We respond to gestures with an extreme alertness and, one might say, in accordance with an elaborate and secret code that is written nowhere, known by none, and understood by all." In the late 1950s Ekman and Wallace Friesen (among others) began work on cracking that "secret code" by developing a theoretical framework for studying nonverbal behavior that has been utilized by most researchers in the field (1969). That framework includes the following categories:

Gestures that are specific enough to be interpreted or defined, usually in a few words, are precise enough to be given the designation of *emblems*. "OK," "shame on you," "good luck," are typical American emblems. Pointing the finger toward the head may refer to the implication that someone is smart, dumb, or crazy; these emblems usually refer to other people although one can gesture toward oneself.

Gestures that accompany speech and are designed to facilitate one's verbal expression are known as *illustrators*. They are not as specific or explicit as emblems but rather are used to illustrate and/or emphasize what is being said.

Body language can influence the give and take in conversation by encouraging someone to continue speaking, or to become more interesting, or to give the other speaker a chance to talk. In this instance, the hands seem less important than the movements of head and eyes. These gestures are designated as *regulators*. It seems that these are more automatic and, therefore, more difficult to inhibit or restrain primarily because they are more outside our general awareness, like involuntary habits.

Over the years, these categories of emblems, illustrators, and regulators have served well to facilitate the description of body movements that accompany speech. More recently, however, gestures have been described as being more complex and more consistent with current thinking about brain function. This new way of looking at gestures also relates more closely to the material presented in this book.

David McNeill, professor of linguistics and psychology at the University of Chicago, writes:

> *Gestures exhibit images that cannot always be expressed in speech, as well as images the speaker thinks are concealed. Speech and gesture must cooperate to express the person's meaning. A conception of language and gesture as a single integrated system is sharply different from the notion of 'body language'—a communication process utilizing signals made up of body movements, which is regarded by its believers as separate from and beyond normal language. This concept is the product of an excessively narrow analysis, just as is the traditional linguistic notion of a spoken language as exclusively comprising a system of speech sounds plus a grammar.*

> *With these kinds of gestures people unwittingly display their inner thoughts and ways of understanding events of the world. These gestures are the person's memories and thoughts rendered visible. They belong…to the inside [world] of memory, thought, and mental images (1992, pp. 11-12).*

His point, then, is that language has two components, one spoken and one illustrated, which would be consistent with the idea that speech is formed in the left half of the brain and spacial concepts and images in the right half of the brain. (See Chapter 5, "Body Sides and Brain Hemispheres.")

While McNeill thinks the term *body language* presents too constricting a concept; nonetheless it has entered common parlance and really serves quite well because of its general utility. His objection to the term aside, his contribution has been to expand the concept of body language from being seen as an "add on" feature to being as inherently linguistic as speech.

Self-Touching

Studies of body movement in which the hand is brought to the body are limited in number and scope. Attention to this form of nonverbal communication has been traditionally slight, and we have far fewer designations and much less precise terminology for self-touching than we have for gestures. But we touch ourselves frequently, far more often than we realize. Self-touching particularly has been depicted in several ways.

Autistic Gestures

In the 1930s Maurice Krout at the Chicago Psychological Institute was among the first to research self-touching, and hypothesized that "conflict was of the essence of the inner process." Using an experimental procedure, he attempted to induce a feeling state by presenting his subjects with a challenge that was inherently conflictual. Krout postulated that the motions that resulted would in themselves symbolize the emotion. He ultimately believed the research tended to validate this supposition that a "collision of impulses," that is, internal conflict, brought about self-touching (1954).

Because these movements are not directed toward others but are self-directed, they are, he wrote, "unwitting or non-conscious responses *whose symbolism must be captured and translated before they can be understood or verbally defined.*"[5] To describe this concept, he chose to use the term *autistic gestures*, which did not survive as a clinical term perhaps because it is not quite accurate; these motions are not idiosyncratic but are similar or even identical from person to person and, in fact, are not gestures as commonly defined.[6]

Krout observed that the difference between conventional gestures and autistic gestures was the ability to interpret them verbally:

> *Autistic gestures are adaptive as well as expressive, but they are always nonverbal, and cannot be interpreted verbally....Autistic gestures are adaptive because they drain off impulses and hence are tension-reducing; not because they affect the responses of another to oneself. In other words autistic gestures constitute a form of self-communication* (1954).

Krout did not propose an explanation for the mechanics of autistic gestures and concluded this study with the development of a long list of emotional states. This material, however, did not lend itself readily to clinical or personal application.

---

[5] Italics mine.
[6] Autism is defined as "the tendency to view life in terms of one's own needs and desires...unmindful of objective reality."

Adaptors

Ekman and Friesen categorized self-touching as *adaptors*[7] (1972, p. 361). Knapp, in reference to their work, observes that adaptors:

> *are perhaps the most difficult to define and involve the most speculation. They are labeled adaptors because they are thought to develop in childhood as adaptive efforts to satisfy needs, perform actions, manage emotions, develop social contacts, or perform a host of other functions…they are fragments of actual aggressive, sexual or intimate behavior and often reveal personal orientations or characteristics covered by verbal messages. Leg movements can often be adaptors, showing residues of kicking aggression, sexual invitation, or flight (1972, p. 6).*

According to Ekman and Friesen, this category includes hand movements that are:

> *relevant to facilitating or blocking sensory input; some are relevant to ingestive, excretive, or autoerotic activity; some are relevant to grooming, cleansing, or modifying the attractiveness of the face and body; some are relevant to facilitating or blocking sound making and speech; and some appear to be aggression directed against the self (1972, p. 362).*

These descriptions include almost every type of self-touching, ranging from non-specific biological needs (e.g., toiletry) to specific responses to feelings and situations. The authors do not consistently address why these actions occur, short of being adaptive. Also, this category does not always include the context in which the body action occurs.

---

[7] They also noted, "Rosenfeld called this category *self-manipulations*, Mahl called it *autistic*, and Freedman and Hoffman called it *body-focused*. All agree this behavior is related to negative feelings."

If the term *adaptors* is limited to the category of nonspecific tension-releasing, usually repetitive motor movements, then they are readily distinguished from the personal body language described in this book. Perhaps the best indicator of an adaptor, used in this sense, is its idiosyncratic nature. That is, it is more of an habitual response of a particular individual when under stress, such as a rocking movement of the body or repetitive movements, as of one's crossed leg or foot. We might also think of individuals who routinely use suggestive or even sexual movements or postures when facing certain types of social stressors. Not only are these adaptors usually less discreet and specific than personal body language, but often persist longer than other indicators of specific conflictual states.[8]

Although I believe the original category of adaptors was overly inclusive, I concur with Ekman and Friesen's conclusions about some body motions that relate to the type of self-referential touching described in this work. "We believe," they write, "that specific types of self-adaptors are *associated with specific feelings and attitudes*."[9] In this respect, they describe some adaptors that illustrate this specificity:

> *Picking or squeezing part of the body is aggression against the self or aggression towards others temporarily displaced onto the self; covering the eye with a hand is relevant to preventing input, avoiding being seen, and shame. Both the action and location of the self-adaptor must be considered to decode the specific meaning of the act, although certain actions...may have meaning in themselves.*

---

[8] This is not fully reliable, however, in that some personal body language as a sign of specific conflict may persist as long as the stimulus is present; i.e., there is a protracted sense of conflict.

[9] Italics mine.

While many parts of the body can perform an adaptor action (lips, teeth, legs, feet) we will discuss here only self-adaptors in which the hand is performing the action in contact with some part of the body....Our list of locations which the hand may contact is based on both biological and psychological functions associated with different parts of the body. For example, we distinguish the eyes, ears, nose, and mouth, but do not make locational distinctions within the cheek. While we make no distinctions within the forehead, we do distinguish the temple because it can symbolize thought.

They continue by saying that specific types of self-adaptors "may be triggered by the motives or affects which are being verbalized, or by discomfort or anxiety about conversation....All other things being equal," they conclude, "self-adaptors occur more frequently when the person is in a private rather than a public place...[but] no matter when it occurs, the adaptor is never deliberately employed to communicate information to another person" (1972, pp. 362-363).

These important studies by Ekman and Friesen constitute a preliminary attempt to decode this significant aspect of body language. They moved on to other areas of study and, to the best of my knowledge, did not rigorously pursue study of the movements they referred to as adaptors. (In further work, Ekman titled this category *manipulators*.) Like Krout, Ekman and Friesen were pioneers in body language research, but this area of their work did not lend itself to practical application and hence has not found its way into clinical or popular use.

Deception and Leakage

In prior studies, self-touching as a form of body language has been seen by researchers primarily as a clue to deception and lying.[10] In the sense that self-touching inadvertantly signals attempts at deception, it has been referred to as *leakage*. For some researchers, leakage refers to any clue to deception. While agreement exists among students of body language that deception is always involved, the material in this book is presented with the view that personal body language always includes an element of *self-deception*—that is, there is a lack of internal congruence.

Ekman distinguishes between deception clues, i.e., when a liar's behavior suggests lying without revealing the truth, and leakage, when a liar mistakenly reveals the truth. He notes the belief that people fidget or make restless movements when they are ill at ease or nervous is well substantiated, but also notes these movements are not reliable indicators of lying. Studies by other individuals have concluded the opposite, namely that although a decreased frequency of simple gesticulations with hands occurs, an increased frequency of hand to face self-touching and body shifts is evident. Ekman speculates the disparity might be related to the importance of what is at stake in the mind of the person lying. He also notes that individuals tend to have a particular type of deception clue that is their hallmark, whether it is twisting a ring, picking cuticles, or twisting a moustache (1992, Chapter 2).

Desmond Morris includes a lengthy description of leakage in the book *Manwatching*. "Most of us can be classified as Leakers..." he writes.

---

[10] While the terms lying and deception have been used interchangeably, in this work they are not, as deception is often not consciously intended.

"The cooperative lie…plays a major role in many social engagements."
He then cites a "devious minority group":

> *Professional Non-leakers…those whose working lives involve repeated and prolonged deceptions and, what is more, deceptions that are open to challenge. Unless they are capable of lying successfully and of sustaining their lies, they are doomed to failure in their chosen professions…. I am not thinking…merely of the obvious examples—great actors and actresses—but also…the professional diplomats and the politicians…the lawyers…the confidence tricksters…and the used-car salesmen….For all these, lying is a way of life, a superb skill that is polished…until it sparkles so brightly that the rest of us most of the time actually enjoy being taken in by it* (1977, p. 108).

"Several observers have noticed," writes Morris, "that nose touching and deceit go together in a remarkable way, but no one has ventured to suggest why this should be." In many situations, he says, the finger touches the nose not because an individual is about to lie, but because the question is a complicated one the subject has to think about carefully before answering. He concludes that the nose touch is not simply a sign of lying but is "a reflection of the fact that a split is being forced between inner thoughts and outward actions…which causes us to be deceitful but we cannot be said to be lying [as] there is more to dishonesty than uttering falsehoods….*What [leakage] really shows…[are] thoughts and actions mismatching at a moment of tension.*"[11] His explanation, then, is that these common self-touches are manifestations of deceit, implying that they are fueled by inner conflict (1977, pp. 110-111).

---

[11] Italics mine. Morris popularized the topic of nonverbal communication, making it user-friendly for the general public, often relying on his keen observations rather than research methodology.

The many self-touching movements that have been described as indicators of lying have proven to be unreliable in that they may simply indicate the anxiety about the subject matter or about being challenged or questioned, which can be confused with anxiety about being caught in a lie. Obviously, deception is a complex phenomenon as the degree of conscious awareness and premeditation is quite variable, and thus it has been difficult to ascertain the signals that are specific to the kind and degree of deception.

As researchers have pointed out, the better liars have learned to control the physical signals of purposeful and conscious lying, particularly in reference to the head and upper body. The signals of deception, however, may still be seen in the movements of the legs and feet, which receive less attention in this regard both by the observer and the person lying. Highly accomplished poker players may show no body movement at all when purposefully deceiving. Autonomic responses would still be an indicator of emotional arousal, but even these can be controlled to a certain degree, except pupillary dilation which is the least controllable visible autonomic indicator.

Self-Intimacies

A third approach, elaborated particularly by Morris, has been to term most self-touching[12] as *self-intimacy*, which he says "accounts for the majority of all touching actions that we direct toward ourselves. Self-intimacies can be defined as movements that provide comfort because they are unconsciously mimed acts of being touched by someone else..." (1977, p. 102). In this type of action, individuals stroke or caress

---

[12] He uses the term *auto-contact* to encompass all types of self-touching.

themselves, comfort themselves, or in privacy derive sexual pleasure from genital stimulation of themselves. Sometimes it is seen as the kind of comforting one might have received as an infant or young child, as hugging oneself, or sitting in a posture in which a leg is drawn up and held to the body, which is a particularly female posture. Observing patients with chronic illness in mental institutions, persistent self-intimacies of a severely regressive type occur commonly in both genders.

Self-intimacies are not easily confused with Kinoetics as they are part of grooming and comforting and thus occur daily. Self-intimacies are more prolonged and involve larger motor movements and are easily distinguished from the kind of personal body language that is depicted in this work.

In Sum

This ubiquitous phenomenon of self-touching has been approached by a limited number of researchers in different ways, although not in the fashion described here. Krout and Ekman and Friesen, however, explored core themes that will be developed in this work, and drew attention to the notion that conflict and tension bring about a body response that is adaptive, made in an attempt to restore equilibrium in the body.

Krout, in particular, recognized conflict as provoking specific self-touching movements and attempted to correlate the movements with feelings. He was convinced as a result of his research that the movements were specific and also symbolic, which meant they could be interpreted, and that there were always associated feelings.

Ekman and Friesen also recognized that there could be substantive meaning to some body motions, rather than being simply random actions, and observed that some types of self-touching were associated with specific feelings and attitudes. While clearly their descriptions indicate they saw that many of the touches had meaning, i.e., they were at least unconsciously purposeful, they stopped short of suggesting that touches of this type constituted a well-defined category with symbolic meaning that formed a language.

Ekman and Friesen emphasized an important concept found not only in the study of body language but in general biology and evolutionary history—that is, all organisms are attempting to adapt to their environments at all times. This includes not only the external but also the internal environment, where the basic physiological concept of homeostasis is that of constant attempts at equilibration and balance.

The psyche is a self-regulating system that maintains its equilibrium just as the body does. Every process that goes too far immediately and inevitably calls forth compensations. In this sense we can take the theory of compensation as a basic law of psychic behavior.

- C.G. Jung

Chapter 3

Conflict

Oppositional qualities exist within all of us, and oppositional "truths" compete with one another throughout our lives. We continually experience that, on the one hand, we believe "this" and, on the other hand, we believe "that." Daily life itself seems to present, almost force upon us, one situational conflict after another, and the internal tension of our moral and philosophical poles causes most people to acknowledge that there are areas of their lives about which they feel continually conflicted.

*For the good
that I would
I do not;
but the evil
which I would not,
that I do.*

- The Bible: Romans

Conflicts inherent in our personal and social lives, as well as those prevailing in our culture, include (among others) struggles between skepticism and faith, between the desire to act and the need to contemplate, between the quest for personal autonomy and the desire to be part of the group. If we want what others want, the conflict created is proportional to its availability, e.g., there is only one "first place." We see the need to be objective but our innate subjectivity gets in the way. We wish to forgive a friend a trespass, yet we maintain a grudge. With such a multitude of inner and outer conflicts, there is an underlying sense that our lives will never be peaceful.

All of us experience pull in different directions from the earliest years— for example, whether to please a parent or follow a desire to please oneself in some contrary way. Or somewhat later, we may be pulled between the desire to do well in school and do the associated work, versus the desire to have fun and be with friends. We often tell ourselves we will do one thing, only to find we do another. We make resolutions, even commitments, only to break them.

Conflict is productive of tension and anxiety, which are in turn proportionate to the degree and duration of the conflict. Anxiety differs from fear in that it does not have a readily identifiable source; i.e., it lacks specificity and can come from a sense of being threatened from without or contrarily subverted from within. Psychologist Rollo May believed that anxiety arises from being torn between expectations and contrasting realities, provoking social dilemmas and irresolvable contradictions.

Whereas fear diminishes fairly rapidly when the fearful object is removed or the fearful situation terminates, anxiety persists at least as long as the conflict is operative and unresolved—and as the conflicts are often unconscious, and therefore often unresolved, anxiety can become an habitual state.

Thus, much constant and mostly unconscious internal tension resides in our psyches relating to our experience of desires and feelings that are unacceptable to ourselves and, we believe, to others. Additionally, there are unacceptable parts of ourselves that we don't want to see, or don't want others to see, or believe they don't want to see in us.

An idea basic to psychoanalytic theory is that in order to help relieve psychic tension, we habitually repress certain parts of ourselves that are at odds with other parts. While clinical experience supported this observation since Freud's time up to the present, in recent decades we have graphic evidence of the effect of repression on the brain, as seen in scientific measurements of brain activity and functioning. The implications of the effects of repression in the cause and treatment of mental/emotional disorders are indicated in Chapter 5.

We do not what we ought; What we ought not, we do.

- Matthew Arnold

Development and Conflict

In studying the development of children through various phases of learning and growth, we see how parents shape their behaviors with reward and punishment, encouragement and restriction. The injunctions of the parent are internalized by the child: quiet is good and noisiness is bad; obedience is good, self-assertion is bad; honesty is good, lying is bad.

However, as children attempt to become autonomous, they usually find that these parental guidelines are limiting and experience a stifling of their self-expression; or the rules may seem simply wrong to them—in any case, these injunctions often conflict with their own desires. Consequently, children learn to be deceptive, to hide their transgressions, because they anticipate a negative reaction to those parts of themselves that are feeling opposition to the values of their parents and other authority figures. At an early age, then, we learn that skill at deception is a valuable asset in life and, at times, an invaluable asset—a survival tool in extreme cases. Reflecting on deception, Ekman writes (1992, p. 23), "Lying is such a central characteristic of life that a better understanding of it is relevant to almost all human affairs." He quotes George Steiner (*After Babel*): "The relevant framework is not one of morality but of survival. At every level from brute camouflage to poetic vision, the linguistic capacity to conceal, misinform, leave ambiguous, hypothesize, invent is indispensible to the equilibrium of human consciousness and to the development of man in society."

Who dares think one thing, And another tell.

- Homer

But we are simultaneously confronted with the social, cultural, and often religious requirements to be truthful, which create constant conflict within us. To alleviate the discomfort of being deceptive or to avoid confrontation, we learn to "split," i.e., hide our inner selves from our seen or outer selves. As this continues to occur, our deceptiveness becomes less and less conscious.

Splitting is thus an unconscious response promoted by the need to avoid the recognition by ourselves and others of undesirable, unattractive, unacceptable parts of ourselves, and is supported by the multiple unconscious defenses against anxiety.[1] This is happening even as we develop an ideal self (sometimes referred to as our ego ideal), an image of self that is a combination of what others want to see in us, and the self as we wish it to be seen and to which we aspire. This is the self that we tend to put forward, devoid of those aspects that do not fit or measure up to the ideal, leading therefore to an incomplete presentation of oneself.

Aspiring to an ideal self is not only inevitable but desirable. The problem that often arises in the attempt to achieve this ideal is that we repress the parts of ourselves that don't conform and attempt to "leapfrog" our way to the ideal, rather than acknowledge our limitations and work our way upward. If this occurs, the dichotomy between what we are and what we wish to appear to be results in perpetuating self-deception and represents an unconscious obstacle to our well being and spiritual growth.

Should habituation to splitting as a mode of operating continue from childhood and adolescence into adulthood, it reinforces and perpetuates the dichotomy between the false self presented to the world and the inner self of authentic experience not revealed to others. While splitting in a child's early life helps allay anxiety, in adult life constant disparity between the false or outward self and the true self can actually increase anxiety. Jung's concept of one's *persona,* that is, the mask we display to the world, relates to this notion of splitting as an attempt to manage conflict and alleviate anxiety. As seen in so many cultural settings—

No man, for any considerable period, can wear one face to himself, and another to the multitude, without finally getting bewildered as to which may be true.

- Nathaniel Hawthorne

---

[1] There are 25 recognized defense mechanisms and many more if combinations and permutations are included.

from the dramas of the ancient Greeks to the ceremonies of remote African tribes—masks are used to illustrate the other parts of ourselves and are revealing of a universal awareness of parts and splitting.

The desire to conform, to display an acceptable outer self, to put on the correct mask, is a dominant feature of the human psyche. In a well-known psychological experiment devised by Richard Crutchfield, a group of participants were given tests of visual discrimination, including estimating the length of two lines:

> *The group's individual answers relayed by a signaling system, were so contrived that every subject believed his own estimate to be contradicted by everyone else in the room, so each believed himself alone…in this case everyone showed a marked increase in physiological measures of anxiety. Those who then conformed with the bogus group consensus…lowered their anxiety. Those who called it as they saw it…kept their anxiety high. They lived with anomaly, dilemma, and seeming contradiction.*

Thus, the effort to maintain a true self under external pressure to agree with the consensus produced marked anxiety—their "courage to be" (Paul Tillich) left them unmasked (Hampden-Turner, 1981, pp. 58-59).

The Dimensions of Conflict

As children we learn to talk to ourselves as our parents talk to us, and we continue to have this dialogue throughout our lives so that our "above" (our parent figures, our superego) talks to our "below" (our drives, motives, and desires that are not acceptable). These types of conflict have been depicted by Freud, Jung, and others as being in the *vertical dimension*—the unacceptable parts of us in the below, the supervisory and even dictatorial parts of us in the above, with the ego in the middle trying to deal with both.

We can secure other people's approval, if we do right and try hard; but our own is worth a hundred of it.

- Mark Twain

This vertical schema is the one traditionally used in attempting to understand mental dynamics—the superego above, the ego in the middle, and the instincts or id below. Depth psychology is based on this premise, and the many schools and branches of psychotherapy still utilize this vertical model with variations and additions

Jung, standing apart from the other great early theorists, called attention to other poles within the psychic structure, including thinking/feeling and sensation/intuition. These dimensions can be considered on a *horizontal axis* as, very simply, the polarity between our own left and right sides, left and right brains, our masculine and feminine principles. **This work considers particularly the conflict that plays out on this horizontal stage.** (See "Body Sides and Brain Hemispheres.")

A third vector, *perpendicular* to the vertical and horizontal axes, is the internal/external. Jung called attention to personalities tending to be primarily introverted or extroverted. This axis is not at odds with either of the other two, as all three are operating at all times. For example, a conflict between thinking and feeling may show itself primarily in behavior toward something or someone external, or may manifest exclusively as symptoms of an internal struggle.

The Dynamics of Conflict

Dynamics refers to the science or principles of the driving forces acting in any field. In psychology, it refers to the motivational forces that drive behavior. In biology, the fundamental dynamic is that of approach-avoidance. The survival of all living organisms depends upon this basic behavioral mechanism. Even the amoeba has some kind of awareness that one stimulus is useful and is to be sought after, while another stimulus is noxious and is to be avoided. Thus, even a one-celled organism knows when to advance and when to retreat, presumably responding

The difficulty in life is the choice.

- George Moore

to the basic forces of attraction and repulsion. Humans and other higher creatures are certainly assisted in survival behavior by the consciousness, derived through experience, of pleasure and pain—both of which serve as adjuncts to approach and avoidance.

When we are confronted with environmental stimuli that cause the mechanism of approach and avoidance to operate simultaneously, conflict ensues. The result of such a situation is an initial movement in one direction, most often approach, until something within prevents us from moving further toward the intended goal. When the route of approach or, more particularly, the route of avoidance is blocked, we will experience even greater conflict, whether we are conscious of it or not. As conflict is inherent in the approach-avoidance mechanism, it is thus an essential part of the human condition, which enables us to appreciate it as an alert to change direction or modify behavior.

*Of evils
we must choose
the least.*

- Aristotle

In addition to the simple approach-avoidance situation, conflict is also experienced in double approach or double avoidance. When there is more than one desirable goal but only one can be pursued, the problem is with what we might call *over-choice*. Similarly, a person may be faced with more than one unpleasant alternative, which we refer to as a *dilemma*. When we are on the "horns of a dilemma," neither choice is acceptable, and we attempt to choose the lesser of two evils.

The self-referential motions described in this work occur *in response to this sense of internal conflict*,[2] and whether or not it is perceived to be with

---

[2] Observations made by other authors and researchers in the field, notably Krout, indicate that indeed conflict is at the heart of this self-touching phenomenon. See "Body Language: *A Brief Overview*."

someone/something outside oneself, the conflict is ultimately always within us—that is, the approach-avoidance mechanism is always operational in conflict.

Beyond Conflict

Conflict is always manifested by a stress response, however slightly perceptible. If one continues to ignore a body response, it becomes less noticeable. The resultant decrease in sensitivity to the sense of discomfort leads to an individual's failure to appreciate the existence of conflict, thereby making resolution improbable. Conversely, increased attention to the body's signals heightens awareness and increases the chance of conflict resolution, with the associated lowering of stress and increase in peacefulness.

Conflict is particularly difficult to resolve when it is at the unconscious level. The first stage of conflict resolution, then, is *awareness of conflict*; the second stage is the ability to *recognize the nature of the conflict*. The third stage is the ability to *tolerate the anxiety* that comes with being host to opposite or contradictory notions, values, beliefs—to accept living with, in fact, being the paradox. The last stage is to learn to *be at peace with the paradox* and move toward integrating the polarities.

If one accepts the premise that self-referential touching represents a manifestation of inner conflict or negativity, then a lack of self-touching (if not motivated by restraint, defensiveness, or secretiveness) would indicate someone without internal conflict—someone with a state of mind that is peaceful or balanced.

Those who honestly mean to be true contradict themselves more rarely than those who try to be consistent.

- Oliver Wendell Holmes

In the posture of the unconflicted person, there would be no inference of defensiveness, resistance, or opposition. Instead, it would indicate balance and centeredness. Perhaps the statues representing the Virgin Mary, in which the posture is open and accepting of her fate, has a universal appeal for just that reason. Bringing the hands together, as in prayer or respect, also indicates balance and peace, just as it facilitates integration and cooperation between the sides.

The yogi sits in the lotus position in meditation, cross-legged, arms extended outwardly, hands resting on the knees. It seems that adopting this position of openness and receptivity creates balance and reduces the ever-present sense of conflict. In this position, with a combination of focused breathing and vibrational sounds, a response is noted at the neurophysiologic level, as the brain waves slow and the brain hemispheres become synchronized. The electroencephalogram (EEG) is able to register this physiologic balance, showing decreased left hemispheric dominance, increased right hemispheric activation, and slowing of the predominant beta rhythm (13-20 cps) to alpha (8-12 cps). The individual notes a feeling of relaxation and peacefulness, and—with practice—enters an altered state. One might think of this integrated state as beyond conflict.

To be whole persons we must get ourselves off our hands.

- Harry Emerson Fosdick

Memory—that strange deceiver!
Who can trust her? How believe her—
While she hoards with equal care
The poor and trivial, rich and rare.

- Walter de la Mare

Chapter 4

Kinoetics: *Our Personal Body Language*

The experience of internal conflict is discomforting. The discomfort may be so slight that the sensation can be ignored at the conscious level, or it may be experienced simply as a sense of increased awareness of that part of the body. The distress can also be noted as pressure or heaviness and frequently is experienced as an itch. Occasionally, the sensation is even felt as pain. In the Kinoetic response, the hand is brought to the area of the body that is registering distress, and generally we experience that touch as comforting. We may wonder why the hand is sensed as comforting and why this effect is felt at some parts of the body more than others. We may also wonder why this response occurs at all and what purpose it serves.

The significance of these Kinoetic responses is more easily ascertained in the respectful and confidential setting of psychotherapy and likely requires such a specialized setting for studying these responses. Yet even in such a favorable context and even as an individual is consciously and with all deliberation striving for self-disclosure, resistance manifests and intellectual defense mechanisms kick in, blocking conscious awareness of the full nature of the conflict.

Nonetheless, in spite of the operation of these defenses, it appears that the need of the unconscious to express itself results in a bodily response to the unresolved conflict, and the person responds by touching herself, signaling the presence of repressed aspects of this mental/emotional conflict. At those times, if an individual is asked why she has touched her chest or arm or leg, the reply is often,*"I just had an itch."* But it is just as likely that she has no explanation and can only acknowledge that *her hand seemed drawn to that part of the body.*

The unquiet heart and brain.

- Tennyson

When an individual is experiencing and registering conflict with body movement, it is generally the hand that makes contact with some part of the body, most frequently the face and head. A terrible thought, for example, precedes an awareness of sensation registering on the head with the result that the hand moves in response to this internal cue and touches an area on the head. A delay may be perceived between the thought and the movement, part of which is due simply to the time it takes for the hand to reach the body—which seems to be a long period relative to the perception of thought as instantaneous.

Because of this delay, an individual who is not attuned to the significance of this personal body language might not be aware of the connection between rubbing an itchy eye and the thought producing the sensation. Often, by the time we have responded with the hand, the thought has passed and we have moved on to another thought. However, if we repeatedly attend to this experience, we note that the thought and sensation are virtually simultaneous, and that part of the delay in registering feeling in the body is the *acquired diminution of sensitivity to the body experience*; i.e., most people have become variably desensitized to their feelings ("not tuned in").[1]

The Kinoetic response happens *automatically* in reaction to the complex of thought and emotion. Emotional states, felt in the body and recorded in the brain, are essential for the development of mind as we know it. The body, then, is an integral part of mind serving as the source of information and background for all mental activity—or the mind's "ground reference" (Damasio, 1994, pp. 223-235; *Descartes' Error* is recommended reading for those interested in this topic).

When the heart aches, all members partake of the pains.

- Cervantes

---

[1] As we have all observed, individuals vary widely in their degree of sensitivity and responsiveness to physical sensations.

Thus, *the mind* is not distinct from *the body* and is present not only in the brain but in all aspects of the body in its functioning. One could say that personal body language is a recall in the body/mind in response to the brain/mind, making a connection between the thought or memory and where it registers in the body.

In my mind's eye, Horatio.

- Shakespeare

In the first half of the 17th century, Rene Descartes separated mind and body in a philosophical system that involved a set of natural laws or fundamental properties. (He put off publishing his first work due to the political climate at the time, as he saw what happened to Galileo at the hands of the Church after he had shared his revolutionary scientific concepts with the world.) Once separated, the reunion of mind and body has taken three centuries, as the Cartesian model appealed to science for an extremely long time. Even today, an extreme polarity exists among scientists regarding *mind*,[2] but general agreement indicates that the brain and body function as a unit, acting synergistically, with constant interchanges of information via feedback loops.

I have said that the soul is not more than the body. And I have said that the body is not more than the soul.

- Whitman

Feedback loops in the body have been studied extensively in both the areas of function (physiology) and underlying biochemistry. Examples include the observation that when one muscle contracts (e.g., the flexor muscles such as the biceps), its opposite (in this case the triceps) must relax for smooth functioning to occur. At a more subtle level, insulin secretion is dictated by the body's perception of an elevated blood sugar level; conversely, sugar (glucose) is released from glycogen stores in liver and muscle in response to a low sugar level.

The Kinoetic response involves feedback at several levels: at an energetic level not easily measured; at a chemical level, when neurotransmitters

---

[2] The differing positions range from the idea that mind is solely the product of the brain, to the idea that the mind informs and shapes the body and brain—although the body, particularly the brain, in turn continues to shape the mind.

are released in the area of the body experiencing sensation; and at the level of the central nervous system, where sensory and motor loops carry impulses from the skin or viscera through nerves and the spinal cord to the brain. These impulses are then carried back along similar pathways to muscle groups in a coordinated and complex pattern. Thus, feedback loops work from the most subtle level, e.g., that of thought, through all energetic levels of the body, ultimately manifesting in group muscle activity which is *expressed in the body's patterned language.*

The skin over the viscera is supplied by nerves from the same spinal segments that supply the organs and glands directly, providing a pathway for a person to experience sensations associated with those viscera. In addition to the "classical" nervous system, evidence suggests that more than one mode of energy transmission exists in the body. Other modes include the ancient concept of *meridian energy flow*, which serves as a basis for acupuncture treatment in Oriental medicine; the *direct current (DC) system* (Becker, 1985; Becker, 1990), which may be the primary mode of energy transmission in humans (as in lower organisms); the vibrational effect of *waves*, those generated within the body which extend through the skin and beyond (where they can be measured, as by an MRI), and the notion of *waves* external to the body and having an energetic effect on it. *Chi*, considered in the East to be the fundamental energy of the universe, is presently immeasurable.

Perhaps most pertinent to Kinoetics is the concept of *fields*, that is, those areas surrounding electrical and magnetic events in which their effects can be detected, even at a distance. Fields in the body range in strength from the small level, e.g., of the atom, increasing in magnitude through an aggregation of cells, tissues, and organs, culminating in the internally generated field of the body itself. An external personal field, called the *auric field* for millennia in the East and the *morphogenetic field* in the West, will likely someday be accessed by science.

A man becomes aware of his life's flow.

- Matthew Arnold

To see as far as one may and to feel the great forces that are behind every detail.

- Oliver Wendell Holmes

Princess Diana and Elizabeth Dole react in different ways at an international meeting about the damage land mines continue to do around the world. Diana is indicating felt "heart" emotion (see Body), whereas Dole is more "in her head," presumably trying to decide if and how she might influence the outcome. (See Head, and Chin and Jaw).

(AP/Wide World Photos)

Where We Touch

Touching the trunk of the body carries a considerably different significance than touching the head or extremities. While touching any area of the body has symbolic significance, *touching the head or extremities* refers essentially to the *function* of that part. Thus, a finger placed in the ear would indicate not wanting to hear something (as a child might attempt to avoid hearing by putting fingers in both ears), or a hand to the eye would have symbolic reference to seeing or not seeing. Similarly, reference to an arm might indicate the ability to do or not do something, or conflict about willingness to act. Touching the legs might refer to the ability or inability to be mobile, or could refer to the position we take in reference to other individuals or to the world around us.

Touching the trunk of the body usually signals a *troublesome emotion that is affecting that particular area* of the body, as if the emotion or its residue seems stored, stuck, or concentrated there. We intuitively understand this connection. We say such things as, "It broke my heart," "It made me sick to my stomach," "The words stuck in my throat," or "He is a pain in the neck (or arse)." Most people are less aware of sensations in the trunk; touches to that area do not occur with the same frequency as those to the head or limbs.

It is important to add that the *specific* meaning of this personal body language cannot always be ascertained from the movement itself, but a *general* sense of meaning can be inferred with some accuracy by a trained observer. When a self-referential touch is combined with information conveyed by the facial expression and questions or prompts about the topic under discussion (if the person is talking or is willing to share the associated thoughts), the accuracy of the inference is significantly enhanced. *Thus, the context of the motion is ultimately the determining factor in understanding the meaning of the movement, including also whether the movement even has meaning.*

And I am sick at heart.

- Shakespeare

Chapter 5

Body Sides and Brain Hemispheres

Exploring the Horizontal Axis

Protagoras asserted that there were two sides to every question, exactly opposite each other.

- Diogenes

Years ago I noted while observing patients in therapy that they frequently changed physical position when the subject under discussion led to an "on the other hand" focus, belief, or attitude. This observable shift seemed to represent the internal dialogue and, at times, the debate between competing perspectives and values. It became apparent that this was likely due to a switch in dominance from one brain hemisphere to the other.

Although there are many indicators as to which brain hemisphere is more dominant in addressing an issue (that is, which hemisphere is more active), clinical observations provide strong evidence that the position of the body in the chair, particularly the position of crossed legs and also the tilt of the body or head, are the more reliable and obvious indicators. (Recall that each hemisphere of the brain serves the opposite side of the body.) For example, if the hand that is on the same side as an uppermost crossed leg is the more active, that hand motion supports the concept that the individual is speaking particularly from that side. Should the hand on the opposite side to the top leg become active, it indicates that a "conversation" is going on between the two brains, each side with its own point of view and accompanying perspective. As these points of view can differ substantially, they are potentially *conflictual*.

I learned that a different perspective on the subject being discussed *could often be elicited* by suggesting that a person change his physical position if he seemed to be in conflict but was not representing both sides of the conflictual issue equally. Thus, the differing perspectives and the resulting conflict between the two hemispheres of the brain are demonstrated by our personal body language, which in turn reveals unconscious elements that are operative.

An actual example was that of a person talking about why he could no longer be married, giving various reasons. He then began to *contradict* himself by explaining the reasons he should stay married. At the point of contradiction, the most striking physical change was the shift in position in the chair from one side to the other, accompanied by uncrossing and recrossing the legs. At the time of the switch in point of view, the hand on the opposite side of the body (left) moved to indicate "stay married," although initially the motion when presenting the problem occurred with the right hand.

When the conflict produces self-referential touching, as described in Chapter 4, it most commonly involves just one hand (side) acting, a signal that one side is responding to the conflict and, in a sense, is attempting to deal with the issue "at hand." The response is complex— which hand is touching, on which side (the same or opposite), and where—involving the relationship and degree of hemispheric balance in any individual confronted with choice who is attempting to resolve the impasse or negotiate the difference. As to which hemisphere is temporarily in charge, or to use Robert Ornstein's phrase "who's running the show" (1997, p. 176), depends on many factors including the evocative stimulus, hemispheric specializations, and habituation, all of which vary from person to person and event to event.

The truth itself has not the privilege to be spoken at all times and in all sorts.

- Montaigne

If you do not listen to your own being, you will have betrayed yourself.

- Rollo May

Perspectives from the Past

*The Sphinx
With her enigma.*

- Sophocles

Both religious and cultural notions about the significance, primarily symbolic, of the right and left sides of the body and how they differ, preceded by millennia the scientific discovery of the lateralizing features of the brain, which explained the brain's inherent preferences for choice and function of the sides. Cultural notions about right/male and left/female sides of the body are not only about the *qualities* we associate with being male (active, logical, explicit) and female (intuitive, nurturing, connotative), but also refer to *values*. In the Pythagorian tradition of Greece, Ornstein observes "the right was associated with the one, the odd numbers, the light, the straight, the good, and the male, while the left corresponded to the many, the even numbers, the dark, the crooked, the evil, and the female" (1997, p. 83).

*Nature has given
women so much
power that the law
cannot afford to
give her more.*

- Samuel Johnson

Over the centuries, differing values have been ascribed to the masculine and feminine as inferred by the relative importance of gods and goddesses in each culture. But beginning about 4000 years ago, the right/male side of the body began to be seen as having much higher value and importance than the left, a view that has persisted into modern times. The left/female side of the body experienced a devaluation associated with the eventual disappearance of the "Goddess"—that is, the myth or cult of a feminine deity[1] as Mother of All, the life-giver, life-sustainer—from recorded history. What happened to the high valuation of the feminine left side and how did the male right side gain dominance? There remains much speculation about the reason for this shift.

------

[1] She was known as Inanna in Sumer, Isis in Egypt, Asherah in Canaan, Demeter in Greece.

It is not possible to weight all the factors causing this shift, but we must include the developing skill and predominant use of the right side (hand) for tool making, hunting, and warfare. Researchers have taken note of the fact that tools and cave paintings dating from the Stone Age indicate a slight shift from what Ornstein calls "random handedness" to right-hand preference. By the Bronze Age, with its inexorable technological progress in such areas as metallurgy, pottery making, agriculture, and engraving, the right hand had gained dominance across most early societies. (It is interesting that contemporary preliterate cultures, such as those of New Guinea natives, Australian aborigines, and African pygmies, have a higher percentage of left-handers than literate societies although all cultures show a right-hand predominance.)

There is a history in all men's lives.

- Shakespeare

A view offered by Friedrich Engels proposed that a dramatic change in prehistoric times in the relationship between men and women was directly related to the emergence of hierarchies and the increasing premium placed on private property, which came to include women, making way for the "world historical defeat of the female sex." Anthropologist Claude Levi-Strauss was of the opinion that a shift in values occurred when men began to view women as possessions to ensure, among other things, knowledge of the origin of their offspring.

Riane Eisler offers another perspective with formulation of the Cultural Transformation theory to explain the disappearance of the Goddess, writing that "underlying the great surface diversity of human culture are two basic models of society." She refers to one as the *"dominator* model...either patriarchy or matriarchy—*ranking* one half of humanity over the other." The other, "in which social relations are primarily based on the principle of *linking* rather than ranking, may best be described as the partnership model"(1988, p. xvii). Based on archeological study, it was primarily the partnership model that existed during the Neolithic/agrarian period when cooperation took place between the sexes and within the community, and warfare was minimal or absent.

She takes particular note of Crete, where from about 6000 to 2000 B.C. that culture flourished, relying on the power and good graces of the Goddess, even as she was steadily being replaced by warlike male gods—the dominator model—in the rest of the civilized world. "In Crete," she writes, "for the last time in recorded history, a spirit of harmony between women and men as equal participants in life… appears to pervade" (1988, p. 31).

It was also in Crete that Leonard Shlain (1998) developed his thesis about the increased shift to right hand/left brain dominance, with its associated cultural and societal implications. He based his concepts on the singular abruptness of the Goddess' fall, and that it occurred coincidentally with the development of the alphabet in Mediterranean cultures. Finding support in earlier observations by Ornstein, Robert Logan, and others, he provides a cogent argument for the acquisition of literacy—as well as an appreciation for the concept of time—as being responsible for the increased control of the left hemisphere and the transition to an increased valuation in society of the dominating right/male side.

Notions about Handedness

When we speak of the body's left and right sides, the inclination has been to speak of them particularly in noting handedness, with the right hand having more importance. The vast majority of humans are right

'Tis one and the same Nature that rolls on her course, and whoever has sufficiently considered the present state of things might conclude as to both the future and the past.

- Montaigne

handed, with only about 10% being left handed. This contrasts with the lack of side preference in animals, including our primate cousins, so it would seem that human evolution favored—or required—a dominant side or hand.

The significance of the right hand and its dominance has not gone unnoticed in our written history. In Psalm 98 of the Old Testament, God's "right hand has won victory for him,/his holy arm." In the New Testament, Jesus sits at "the right hand of God." In common parlance, someone who is indispensable to us is our "right-hand man."

Carl Sagan wrote, "The upraised and open right hand is sometimes described as a 'universal' symbol of goodwill." He noted that it is the male who traditionally goes to war, carrying and using a weapon, predominantly in his right hand, in an act that is "characteristically male," just as the right-handed gesture of peace, indicating that the warrior is weaponless, is a "characteristically male greeting" (1977, pp. 104-105).

Conversely, over the centuries the left has acquired a negative connotation. The word *gauche,* from the French for *left,*[2] has come to mean socially awkward or tactless. A "left-handed compliment" is one that is ambiguous, and a "left-handed ship" is one that doesn't steer correctly. Interestingly, in sign language the right thumb extended upward means good, but the left little finger means evil. The ultimate insult, however, is probably that the left hand is associated with the performance of unclean acts.

---

[2] In comparison, the French term *droit* means *right* and someone who is described in English as *adroit* is skilled or very capable in some way.

There is no "Bill of Lefts."

- Carl Sagan

It was not for nothing that the raven was just now croaking on my left hand.

- Plautus

In an historical and literary sense, hands are symbolic indicators of the *oppositionality of left and right sides.* Think of the saying from Matthew and attributed to Christ, "Let not thy left hand know what thy right hand doeth"; and before Matthew, Plautus wrote, "In the one hand he is carrying a stone, while he shows bread in the other." There is, of course, the familiar phrase one hears when contrary ideas are juxtaposed, "but on the other hand…."

Asymmetry, Lateralization and Oppositionality

People with symmetrical faces and bodies have a definite advantage in life—in physical prowess (the speed of a runner is directly proportional to the degree of symmetry),[3] and in attractiveness (research indicates attractiveness is created by both the symmetry of the two halves of the face and the proportions of the elements of the face in the ratio of the golden mean, the ratio given us by Pythagoras 2500 years ago). Proportions of the face and body may be more a result of genetic endowment, whereas asymmetry may result as much or more from other factors.

As the movements of each side of the face are controlled by the opposite brain hemisphere, logically a symmetrical face and facial expression reflect balanced activity of the hemispheres, whereas asymmetry of the face implies imbalance of brain hemisphere activity.

Asymmetry thus might seem undesirable, yet it occurs commonly in people and may begin in the human fetus as early as 14 days after conception; it can be the result of many factors including maternal illness and poor nutrition. Additionally, evidence strongly suggests

*The face
of his desire
and the shape
of his dream.*

- Joseph Conrad

---

[3] Research by John Manning, Professor of Biological Sciences, University of Liverpool.

maternal stress may alter brain development in the fetus resulting in persistent mood and personality changes in later life.[4] Also, impairments of bonding between mother and infant will adversely affect the child's emotional state, as well as influence the experience-dependent maturation of the infant's right hemisphere.[5]

As anatomical and functional changes that occur in the hemispheres are reflected in the face, the oppositional aspect of the self is reflected as well, in that the face registers and expresses emotions differentially. Most people have asymmetry of the face—that is, the two sides don't match. This is best demonstrated by a composite picture in which one side of the face is flipped over and combined with itself. Using this mirror-image technique, Dr. Werner Wolff is quoted in the book *Reading Faces* as noting:

> *a duality of expression in the two halves of the face….The expression of the left face was usually different from the original, obscured by the dominating right expression. It was noticeable that most of the subjects projected their wish images upon this left part of the face, while the expression of the right part referred more to their real personality.*

Wolff proposed that the left side of the face is generally considerably more expressive of our inner self than the right. The authors go on to say, "It has been suggested that the left side is the more 'private' face, the right side a more 'public' façade. It is also true that the right side usually looks more like the whole face than the left side" (Bellak & Baker, 1980, pp. 24-29). Clearly, then, one can have two faces; the enigma of Mona Lisa's smile perhaps is due to the fact that she smiles on one side.

One…that can put on two several faces, and look his enemies in the face with as much love as his friends.

- Samuel Pepys

---

[4] Peter Nathanielsz is Director of the Laboratory for Pregnancy and Newborn Research, Cornell University.

[5] Allan Schore is Assistant Clinical Professor of Psychiatry and Biobehavioral Sciences at UCLA Medical School.

Hemispheric Differences

For differences between the brain hemispheres to become apparent, they had to be studied separately. This was accomplished by cutting the bridge (called the corpus callosum; see page 63) between the two sides of the brain and studying the result. Roger Sperry began that research in the early 1950s on cats and monkeys and was ultimately rewarded with the Nobel Prize in medicine (1981) for this pioneering split-brain work.

I do perceive here a divided duty.

- Shakespeare

Joseph Bogen, a neurosurgeon particularly concerned with attempting to stop intractable epileptic seizures, was aware of Sperry's work and decided to perform the commissurotomy, i.e., to split that bridge between the right and left hemispheres, on severely affected patients. He enlisted Sperry's cooperation in making this decision and in studying the patients both before and after this surgery. Concerning this research, Sperry's fellow research psychologist, Michael Gazzaniga, remarked (1967, pp. 119-124), "From the beginning, one of the most striking observations was that the operation produced no noticeable change in the patients' temperament, personality or general intelligence." He went on to say, however, "close observation…soon revealed some changes in the patients' everyday behavior," such as favoring the right side of the body, and rarely showing spontaneous activity or response to stimulation on the left side. Additionally, "when an object was placed in his left hand he generally denied its presence" and, when blindfolded, he was unable to name it.

Gazzaniga noted:

> *Taken together, our studies seem to demonstrate conclusively that in a split-brain situation we are really dealing with two brains, each separately capable of mental functions of a high order. This implies that the two brains should have twice as large a span of attention and should be able to handle twice as much information—as a normal whole brain.*

Processing and utililizing that information in the absence of whole-brain function, however, would be quite another matter.

Sperry (1966) noted the most far-reaching implication of his work:

> *Everything we have seen so far indicates that the surgery has left these people with* **two separate minds, that is, two separate spheres of consciousness.** *What is experienced in the right hemisphere seems to lie entirely outside the realm of experience of the left hemisphere. This mental dimension has been demonstrated in regard to perception, cognition, volition, learning, and memory.*[6]

Brain researchers Springer and Deutsch write, "Such speculation naturally leads to the possibility of dual consciousness in the intact, normal brain under certain circumstances" (1981, p. 6).

For a brief period following this type of surgery, the left hand in many patients assumed a life of its own, a phenomenon that Bogen referred to as the Disconnection Syndrome, but also more dramatically called it the Alien Hand Syndrome.[7] The left hand often was not under the control of the individual; it would grab onto things and not let go. Particularly dramatic was that the left hand would turn against the person herself. Bogen and others noted that individuals who had this surgery often displayed pleasurable emotion in their facial expressions associated with destructive behavior toward the other side of the body, *predominantly the left side of the body toward the right.*

A truant disposition.

- Shakespeare

---

[6] Emphasis mine.

[7] Bogen subsequently decided that he preferred the term Autonomous Hand Syndrome, but his original designation stuck—and it seems appropriate in that the hand is not only autonomous but often acts in a truly foreign, i.e., alien way.

The conclusions drawn from this split-brain work shed light on some previously unexplained cases involving one side of the body attacking the other. Coincidental to his work, Bogen took note of a report in a French medical paper of a patient named Laura who experienced her left hand grabbing her right hand and wrist as she was driving her car, apparently attempting to force the vehicle off the road. An earlier description in medical literature detailed the story of a patient in the early 1900s in Germany who was terrified of being alone, particularly of falling asleep, as she had the experience of trying to strangle herself when she entered a somnolent state.

It was the curse of mankind... that in the agonized womb of consciousness, these polar twins should be continuously struggling.

- Dr. Henry Jekyll

The possibilities of the split-brain phenomenon were nightmarishly portrayed in Robert Lewis Stevenson's novel *Dr. Jekyll and Mr. Hyde*, published in 1886. The story was based on an article he had read in a French scientific journal on the subconscious mind (although not on hemispheric differences) in the late 1860s or early 1870s—about 10 to 15 years before Freud's theories became known to the general and scientific populace. Stevenson wrote to an associate, "Jekyll is a dreadful thing...but the only thing I feel dreadful about is that damned old business of the war in the members." Stevenson implied that a split exists within the mind, implicating the dual character, the dual personality of man. Jekyll and Hyde can be seen as representations of the left and right hemispheres of the brain, competing to the point that each side is strongly dominant for periods of time, during which each side acts out its different values and goals.

While we have much to learn about the two brains and their mostly uneven and often uneasy relationship with each other, there are certain generalizations that can be made about their differing modes of thought and perception, specialization and function.

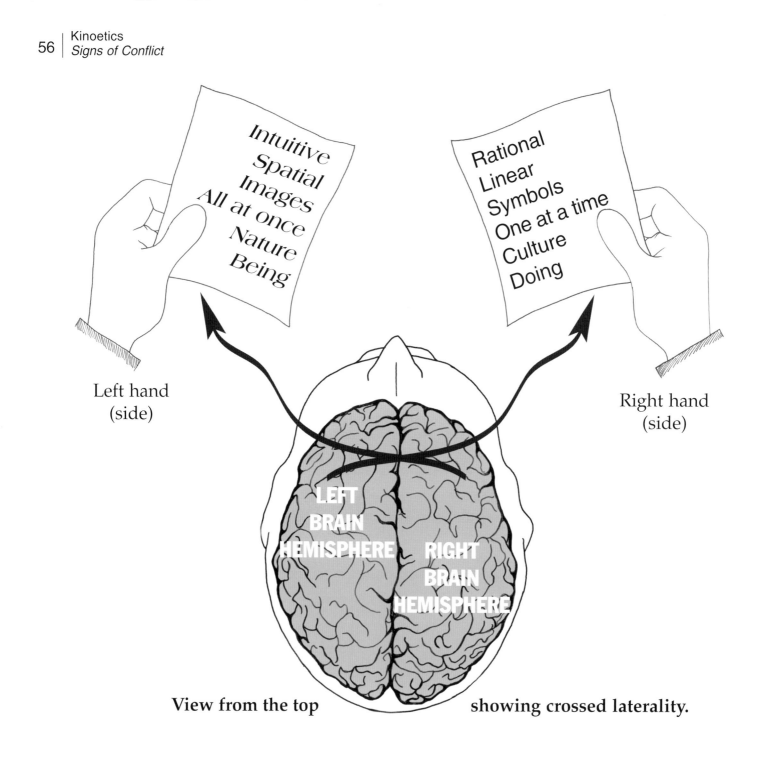

Intuitive
Spatial
Images
All at once
Nature
Being

Rational
Linear
Symbols
One at a time
Culture
Doing

Left hand
(side)

Right hand
(side)

LEFT BRAIN HEMISPHERE

RIGHT BRAIN HEMISPHERE

View from the top   **showing crossed laterality.**

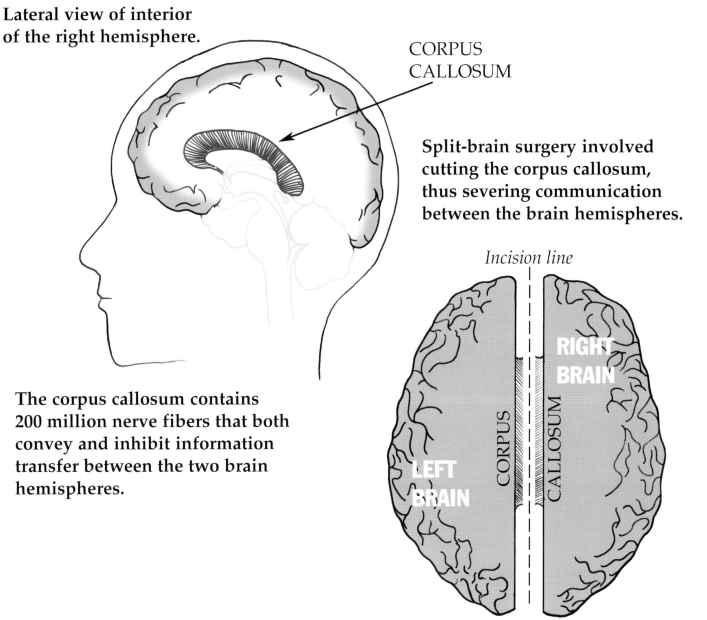

Lateral view of interior of the right hemisphere.

CORPUS CALLOSUM

Split-brain surgery involved cutting the corpus callosum, thus severing communication between the brain hemispheres.

The corpus callosum contains 200 million nerve fibers that both convey and inhibit information transfer between the two brain hemispheres.

Incision line

RIGHT BRAIN

CORPUS CALLOSUM

LEFT BRAIN

Top of brain

The Relationship of Left and Right Brain Hemispheres

The relationship of the two brains is largely determined both by their areas of specialization and the acquired tendency to left brain dominance. The earliest observations about brain laterality, made well over a century ago,[8] were in reference to speech localization in the left brain. When it became apparent in more recent times that spatial tasks were engaged principally in the right brain, the dichotomy of verbal versus spatial functions for a good while characterized the essential differences between the two.

For Springer and Deutsch and other researchers, that dichotomy seemed "too simplistic" to explain all their findings. Rather, "a dichotomy based on different ways of dealing with information in general" was proposed relating to the left brain's superior analytic skills and the right brain's synthetic, holistic abilities.

Shlain notes that the distinctive features of the left hemisphere, which includes doing, numbers, and abstraction, in addition to speech, are linear. He proposes that the left brain evolved into a "new sense organ" to understand the concept of time (Shlain, p. 23). Time, logic, and especially the written word are all understandable as linkages of linear units.

About the right brain, evolutionarily older than the left, he notes:

> *The right brain is nonverbal, and has more in common with earlier animal modes of communication. It comprehends the language of cries,*

Of all the creations of man language is the most astonishing.

- Lytton Strachey

---

[8] In 1936 a county doctor in France, Marc Dax, presented a paper in which he observed that damage to the left brain, but not the right, resulted in loss of speech. In 1864, Paul Broca presented compelling evidence that this was indeed the case.

But what am I?
An infant crying in
the night:
An infant crying
for the light:
And no language
but a cry.

- Tennyson

gestures, grimaces, cuddling, suckling, touching, and body stance. Its emotional states are under little volitional control and betray true feelings....The right brain more often than the left generates feeling states, such as love, humor, or aesthetic appreciations, which are non-logical. They defy the rules of conventional reasoning (pp. 18-19).

The right hemisphere would thus retain its far more ancient and inaccessible, non-logical, and emotional attributes. It remains closely associated with states in which mystery and intuition take precedence over logic, where emotions and allusional imagery hold sway. Many studies indicate that dreaming, one of the great human mysteries, occurs in the right brain.

Left hemisphere: Verbal, rational, analytic, logical, linear, sequential, literal, objective, temporal. Specialist. Manages words, names, numbers, symbols. One at a time. Dislikes surprises, likes certainty. Probabilities. Culture. Doing. Time.

Right hemisphere: Non-verbal, intuitive, synthetic, holistic, simultaneous, spatial, subjective, connotative, nontemporal. "Jill" of all trades. Manages images, faces, metaphors, patterns. All at once. Likes surprises, accepts uncertainty. Possibilities. Nature. Being. Space.

Time & Space
are Real Beings.
A Male & a Female.
Time is a Man, &
Space is a Woman.

- William Blake

About the differing specialties of the hemispheres, Ornstein concludes:

The right side...seems to be specialized for the large elements of perception, the overall shapes of objects, the word shape, the information contained in the size, sounds, and intonation of words strung together. These convey emphases and much of the subtext and contextual meaning. It handles the large movements of the limbs, and the larger emotional reactions such as anger and disgust. And the left side handles the small precise links that carry the smaller, more precise meanings and movements. It's this specialization that contributes to one side being good for the analysis of the small elements versus the synthesis or holistic vision, or language via the literal meaning versus the intonation and indirect meaning. I still like text and context (1997, p. 175).

How wondrous is the brain! How beautifully specialized it is in its dualistic function, which both reflects the duality of the universe and enables us to cope with it.

Hemispheric Organization

The concept of specialization, as described above, should be contrasted with the concept of dominance. Over the years, the terms *hemispheric specialization* and *hemispheric dominance* have been used inter-changeably, but they are different. The areas of specialization of each hemisphere are relatively constant, given an intact brain and a reasonably consistent environment, whereas dominance shifts depending of a number of factors.

Hemispheric dominance refers to the brain that is "in charge" or principally used at any given time. The "choice" of hemisphere to be used in response to a stimulus is related not only to the specialty of verbal versus nonverbal, for example, but also to the type of processing necessary. Anything requiring a narrow focus for processing is a left hemisphere specialty, whereas material requiring a broad focus, such as a stimulus composed of unlike elements or having an emotional association, is a right hemisphere specialty.

Other factors involved in which hemisphere dominates is "whoever gets there first," but also "whoever thinks he/she can do the job." Even though it seems that the special abilities of one hemisphere would be most useful and best equipped to process a certain stimulus, that hemisphere is often disconnected or shut down by the other. If this

Whose even-balanced soul, From first youth tested to extreme old age... Who saw life steadily and saw it whole.

- Matthew Arnold

disconnection proves to be successful at some point, such as enhancing one's sense of self-esteem or by providing a shield from a certain emotional state, it could become the preferred mode of operating and therefore be perpetuated.

Research on disconnection by Gary Schwartz while professor of psychology at Yale University in the 1970s and 1980s, included use of positron emission tomography (PET) scans, brain wave studies, and other technologies. His many studies resulted in finding "repressed people have a functional disconnection between their left and right hemispheres....Years of reliance on this mental defense impeded the flow of information between the right and left sides of their brains" (1996). As the disconnection is functional, that is, not organic or due to injury, it appears to be potentially reversible.

Much may be said on both sides.

- Joseph Addison

Dominance, then, shifts depending on various factors, whereas areas of specialization are relatively constant for Western adults.[9] In recent decades, however, we have become aware that the brain adapts to challenge and necessity, which can cause new neurons to develop (referred to as *plasticity*). Plasticity diminishes with age; e.g., while a young child with damage to one hemisphere may re-learn the compromised ability in the non-damaged hemisphere, this ability diminishes in adults whose brain specialization has become more fixed. Even in adults, however, studies indicate that changing habitual thought and response patterns can change neural maps by growing new neurons and re-routing connections and messaging pathways.

---

[9] Evidence suggests a different configuration may be found in the Japanese brain where intuitive abilities and creative use of space and sound may be largely located in the left brain. The Japanese language, spoken and written, could be the reason for this difference and explain why the Japanese prefer indirect, intuitive thinking and problem solving.

Brain Choice—to Alternate or Integrate

In normal brains, hemispheric dominance cycles from side to side every 90 minutes if unimpeded. A person may override this natural tendency to hemispheric balance by "insisting" on staying in one hemisphere longer, e.g., in the left by reading or the right by enjoying music. At night, however, the whole brain automatically takes over; during dream sleep rapid eye movement from side to side processes events, especially new information and traumatic experiences. This attempt to integrate experiences during dreaming appears to be nature's "re-balancing act" for equal hemispheric participation.

While most activities in which people engage seem to depend upon one hemisphere more than the other, it is noteworthy that professional musicians, especially conductors, have both hemispheres activated. The right hemisphere appreciates the music aesthetically and responds to it emotionally, recognizes it as music and not simply noise; meanwhile the left hemisphere is analytically appraising the musical piece, noting which instruments are playing, the level of proficiency of the players, and quality of the performance generally.

Over 30 years ago, concerning the brain function of most individuals, David Galin wrote that one possibility is that the sides operate in alternation, i.e., take turns (1972, pp. 572-581). Thus, depending on situational demands, when one hemisphere is "on" it would inhibit the other—perhaps even turn it off. It might use some function of the other hemisphere, some part of the other lobe (a "subsystem"), or disconnect the other hemisphere altogether although it continues to be independently conscious. "The fourth possible condition," Galin writes, "in which the two hemipheres are fully active and integrated with each other is the condition that J.E. Bogen and P.J. Vogel associate with creativity, man's highest functioning; unfortunately, this does not appear to occur very often."

Rhythm and harmony find their way into the inward places of the soul.

- Plato

The Corpus Callosum

The bridge between the two hemispheres, the corpus callosum, is a solid-appearing structure once believed to serve the sole purpose of holding the two brains together. It actually consists of two hundred million plus nerve fibers. Worth noting is that women have substantially more of these connecting fibers than men—as many as 20 to 60 million more—suggesting women may have a greater capacity for whole brain thinking, with the ability to access more information and do more than one thing at once. At the same time, perhaps this situation allows women to be more affected by strong emotion.

Can two walk together, except they be agreed?

- The Bible: Daniel

The important discovery that the corpus callosum serves as a medium of communication between the two hemispheres of the brain was momentous, and the split-brain procedures mentioned previously opened up a whole world of brain research as well as proving to be medically useful. *The importance, however, of the subsequent discovery that a significant number of the nerves in the corpus callosum allow* **blocking of information from one brain to the other through inhibitory nerve fibers** *has been vastly underestimated.* That is, each brain has the ability to shut off the other, with different consequences.

The right hemisphere has the capacity to override and at times even completely shut down the left side, as in the case of overwhelming emotion. When a person is "out of his mind with grief," for example, the result is impairment of the left hemisphere's reasoning and judgment capabilities.

The even greater ability of the left brain to shut down the more emotional right likely developed ages ago in response to those dangerous times when the male was engaged in the hunt or in battle, when the need to be highly focused and not distracted by extraneous emotions aided his survival. Without the ability of the left brain to inhibit the right, conflicting goals—for example, to stay and fight or to flee—would leave the combatant ambivalent and jeopardize his safety or that of his family group.

Persisting into the present, the left brain continues to wield the power to shut down the right brain at will (although that propensity seems more prevalent in males) in order to "get on with the fight." The close association of the right brain with the unconscious mind, with its passion, desire for intimacy, and relative unconcern with rules and laws poses significant difficulties for the orderly, regulatory, non-emotional left brain, threatening those aspects of self.

This evolutionary vestige remains even though we do not find ourselves literally stalking prey or staking out territory against warring opponents. We often, however, refer to the modern world as "that jungle out there," and competitive and territorial drives are still largely operative in most societies, eliciting in us a panoply of conflicting emotions that may be disruptive of harmonious balance.

Hemispheric Disorganization

Hemispheric imbalance is implicated in psychiatric disorders including panic disorder, schizophrenia, and obsessive-compulsive disorder (OCD). Interestingly, in common usage, the term "unbalanced" has long been associated with mental disorders.

Anxiety, hostility, and a marked tendency to repetitive thoughts and behaviors result from the increased persistent activation of the left hemisphere. Persistent excessive activation of the right hemisphere results in elated mood, initially with better memory access and expanded attention, but may go on to produce excessive emotional displays.

Things going on at sixes and sevens.

- Goldsmith

OCD, for example, appears to be the result of a markedly overactive left hemisphere and a markedly underactive right hemisphere. The mental and emotional organization and disorganization that is characteristic of people with OCD correspond to the specialized attributes of the left hemisphere. These individuals expend great efforts to process life and problems by a "marked preference for logical, verbal, reasoning approach," as well as difficulty categorizing spontaneously and integrating information, "as revealed by a poor understanding of jokes and metaphors." It seems clear that the underactive right is not able to fully assist by intuition or global processing (Galderisi, Mucci & Maj, 2000, p. 64).

Robert Ornstein observes that when an individual's right lobe is damaged, "it seems to leave the person lacking a sense of what's going on within himself or between the self and the world. This might well be some indication that a sense of meaning of the world in the large sense is what the right hemisphere provides, giving the overview of the person in her world" (1997, p. 175). Galderisi et al conclude that dysfunction of the right hemisphere in particular may represent a common risk factor for psychopathology in general.

The best you get is an even break.

- Franklin Adams

The left/right distinctions run deep into the past of our species....There is every reason to think that the right hemisphere has...misgivings—expressed nonverbally, of course—about the left.

- Carl Sagan

Oppositionality vs. Complementarity

The historic meeting of Cortes and Montezuma…illustrates an improbable encounter of two disparate personalities and civilizations, one literate, controlled by rigid left hemispheric programming and idologies, the other by what Julian Jaynes…called the bicameral mind, presided over by the right hemisphere, the sounding board of the hallucinatory voices of dead kings and immortal gods (Jan Ehrenwald, *Anatomy of Genius*, 1984, p. 174).

SYZYGY: from the Greek—union, pair, yoked together, either alike or opposite.

This quote, provided by the respected brain researcher Robert Ornstein in his excellent book, *The Right Mind*, is meant to illustrate the excess he observes having occurred in areas of education, self-development, and management in the (mis)application of the information available about the differences between the brain hemispheres (pp. 87-115). Ironically, he helped create this situation by his popular writings on the subject. In trying to avoid or reverse "this dichotomania," he seems to miss the opportunity to focus attention on the essential problem posed by these basic differences between the brain hemispheres—their frequent oppositionality—which was so clearly demonstrated in the patients whose brains were split, and which is felt by almost everyone at times as conflictual desires or, worse, as blockages and/or self-sabotage. The quote above actually serves to highlight this oppositionality beautifully.

The evidence suggests that power struggles do take place between the right and left hemispheres pertaining to attitudes, beliefs, motives, and desires that relate to the differing values of each hemisphere. Furthermore, the stronger the emotion attached to any of these elements, that is, the more something is at stake, the more likely the hemispheres are to do battle.

The hemispheres not only have their separate areas of specialization and organization, but each hemisphere is capable of dominating the other—

*There must be,
not a balance
of power, but a
community
of power; not
organized rivalries,
but an organized
common peace.*

- Woodrow Wilson

although usually it is the left that dominates the right. As noted, the key to understanding how this can occur was the discovery that the bridge between them, the corpus callosum, not only had nerve fibers that facilitated communication, but also contained fibers capable of *inhibiting communication* as well, i.e., of shutting off the opposite hemisphere.

Sperry's conclusion that each hemisphere has its own sphere of consciousness and thus can function as an independent entity supports the age-old sense that there are two of us inside, one with predominantly masculine characteristics and one predominantly feminine. Just as two individuals who are in a good marriage, a person's two hemispheres can be well integrated and cooperative with each other, and we recognize this as the partnership model, to use Eisler's phrase. However, if the relationship between the two sides of our brains is contentious and warlike, the dominator model probably holds. That is, just as in a poor marriage, each side is continually attempting to gain the upper hand. Tension results and peace seems unattainable.

In an elegant summary of the challenge presented to us by our evolutionary heritage, Shlain writes (1998, p. 23):

> *Despite our present civilization's far remove from the caves of Lascaux, we remain strongly influenced by the original neurodesign that bred eminently successful nomadic gather-hunters. The dichotomy between the left and right hemispheres mirrors the differences between hunter/killer and gatherer/nurturer strategies.*

Section II

Photo Illustrations

Chapter 6

Introduction to Photo Illustrations

The photos that follow are examples and, of course, do not cover the full range of Kinoetics. These illustrations are intended to provide images to help the reader understand (and recognize) the written material presented in the preceding chapters.

Prior to viewing the illustrations, *your left hemisphere (the male side) has been predominant* in working to decipher the text in a linear mode, making sense of the myriad symbols and managing these symbols in logical sequence. As you look at the photographic images, you simultaneously perceive and synthesize the parts of each image into a recognizable pattern—*you have moved more into the right (feminine) side of your brain.* The illustrations should prove helpful to the reader, as we know that a picture is worth a thousand words.

While this work has emphasized the difficulties that ensue when the hemispheres are not cooperatively engaged, the following combination of photos plus captions invites the participation of both brains. As the image is captured instantly by the right brain, expression of its interpretation in language is a left hemisphere function. Thus, it should be emphasized that the complementarity of the two hemispheres, in spite of their opposing qualities, allows the reader to integrate the written and photographic material for a fuller understanding.

As noted, Kinoetics is a response to a momentary sense of conflict and the motions are therefore usually brief. It is important to remember that a significant percentage of these motions involve not just touching, but rubbing, stroking, or scratching type movements, which cannot be depicted in the illustrations.

Two heads are better than one.

- John Heywood

Most of the illustrations show one hand (side of the body) responding. Recalling that each side of the body is controlled by the opposite brain hemisphere, the indication is that one hemisphere is responding to the conflict and, in a sense, is attempting to deal with the issue, as shown by the associated hand movement. As has been noted, the hand may touch the same side or the opposite side, and as we must also factor in which hand is touching and where, we can see that the response is complex.

At times, the sides of the body are referred to as male and female or masculine and feminine. As noted, these designations have historical precedence, and we know now that the contralateral brain has these associated attributes and values. In practice, reference to the sides of the body and their associated masculine or feminine characteristics works better than referring to the hemispheres (sides of the brain); for with the visible evidence of hand or limb or cheek, it is evident which side of the body is showing signs of conflict.

Symbolism is perhaps most evident in touches to the sense organs. References to seeing have to do with the eyes and the area around the eyes, references to hearing have to do with the ears, references to the mouth have to do with speaking, etc. Touches to the nose, however, most often do not relate to the sense of smell, the obvious reference, but are related to the nose's connection to the limbic system, the seat of the emotional brain. Other areas we reference by touching, as for example the forehead and temple which are historically understood to be the location of perception, ideas, thoughts, and desires, are well-defined and also generally understood in symbolic terms. The symbolism of other areas such as the limbs is less obvious at first, although consideration of structure and function allows the symbolic component to be recognized.

*Truth is the trial of itself
And needs no other touch.*

- Ben Jonson

Of particular importance is the area between the eyes, on either side of the bridge of the nose extending into the inside corner of the eye. This area is significant from the standpoint of meridian operation and balance and thus to whole brain integrity and function. Attempts to avoid feeling or thinking—referred to as repression and denial—will cause disruption of energy flow in this area. (See Eye and Nose.)

The photographs shown in the section on Body illustrate the type of automatic movement of the hand to parts of the trunk that overlie organs, glands, and their fields. Westerners easily understand symbolism based on structure/function as it relates to the sense organs and limbs, but generally don't recognize the functional contribution of organs to emotions. For this it is necessary to turn to Eastern thinking, which has for centuries observed the relationship between viscera and emotional responses.

A note regarding the symbolism: Many times I found the interpretation of a self-referential touch proved a bit of a stretch, causing me to question whether the interpretation was induced or elaborated, rather than truly being expressed by the individual showing a sign of conflict. The repeatedly consistent responses, however, provided and confirmed by one individual after another led me to conclude that the symbolism is, in general, correct.

*He either fears
his fate too much
Or his deserts
are small,
that does not put
it to the touch.*

- James Graham

*I never knew so young a body
with so old a head.*

- Shakespeare

The Head

Mind is the great leveler of all things.

- Daniel Webster

The head, by virtue of housing the brain and carrying four of the principal sense organs and the face, is far and away the most important part of the body.

The human brain, arguably the most wonderful single creation in the universe, is the source and storehouse of thought and is assumed by most people to be the source and location of mind. However, phenomena such as information processing in the body, and perhaps even body memories, suggest that there is mind in the body as well as in the brain.

Because it houses the brain/mind, the head symbolizes consciousness, and reference to the head reflects our sense that it is the seat of awareness. We associate it with our beliefs, our relationship to guidance, authority and power, whether internal or external, and with the positions we take in reference to these issues.

Brain:
An apparatus with which we think we think.

- Ambrose Bierce

The head has always been symbolic of intelligence. A person showing competence is said to have a "good head on his shoulders"; a person of low intelligence who displays incompetence might be referred to as "weak in the head." Someone who is acting irrationally or stupidly may be said to have "a hole in his head." If an individual is unable to utilize his intelligence, i.e., if his efforts are persistently frustrated, we may say he is "beating his head against the wall."

As the head sits at the top of the body and because intelligence and alertness are attributes that often lead to positions of authority, power, or control, *head* is symbolic for anyone who is figuratively "on top"— if we are "head and shoulders" above the crowd, we are better somehow, higher up. The head leads; an individual is the "head of state," "head of a corporation," "head of the family." We lead or "head" ourselves in a particular direction, e.g., we "head" upstream (where we could be "heading" for trouble).

When a person "loses his head" the reference is to the failure of logic and reason to prevail. Beheading as a form of execution is the obvious source for the phrase, where consciousness is extinguished altogether. Conversely, a person's ability to handle difficult challenges may be referred to as "keeping his head." Any situation requiring us to be alert calls for us to be "heads up."

The actual position of the head reflects feelings about an individual's self-worth and in turn his position in relation to others, including God. Someone with justifiable pride and integrity is able to "hold up his head," but shame causes him to "hang his head." A bowed head is associated with grief or receiving a blessing (or, conversely, receiving punishment).

Wherever MacDonald sits, there is the head of the table.

- Emerson

Organizing the Components

Although anatomically the head refers to everything from the neck up, when referring to head we usually mean that larger part of the skull that covers the brain and is in turn (usually) covered with hair. Thus, when we say that a person touched his head, we understand that we are not referring to touching the face or the sense organs. As each component of the head has its own symbolism, each component has a separate section in the illustrations that follow.

Although we think of forehead as a component of the face, it differs symbolically in that the forehead references *mental operations*, as noted in the following section on Forehead and Temple. Most of the face from the brow down, including the eyebrows, is associated with the symbolism of the four senses mediated through eyes, ears, nose, and mouth.

Curiously, while the chin and jaw are at the lower end of the face, not proximate to the brain as is the forehead, they are nonetheless symbolically related to mental operations. Rather than thoughts and memories, however, the chin and jaw relate to *qualities of the will*, which are discussed in the section on Chin and Jaw.

Uneasy lies the head that wears the crown.

- Shakespeare

General Attributes

Touching the head symbolizes conflict concerning an individual's mental activities, such as blocks to receptivity or recognition, or attempts to get it "through" or "into" his head, or where a person is "heading" with his mental activity.

Touching the head also seems to indicate issues about power, or lack of it, and a person's beliefs and attitudes associated with power. A decision about a course of action or a challenge may cause a person to be troubled or puzzled. Subsequently, the position taken is frequently in reference to the use of, or avoidance of, power.

I shall lift my head till it strikes the stars.

- Horace

The top of the head, in particular, seems to reference conflicts about receiving guidance or help, especially from higher sources of power. Historically, the top of the head has been considered in Hindu tradition as the crown chakra and has been associated with receiving guidance, i.e., light or enlightenment. Similarly, the halo around the head in Christian tradition and art reflects those who are "in the light."

Illustrations

1.

The hand at the front center scalp indicates a *block to receptivity*. The motion may occur when one is alone, particularly when attempting some creative enterprise. If it occurs while in discussion with another person, the indication is usually a *lack of receptivity* to input on the topic.

Beyond the utmost bound of human thought.

- Tennyson

2.

When the hand is further back over the top of the head, especially if the hand runs through the hair repeatedly in a stroking manner, there is usually a conflict about *receiving guidance* from another person. Most often, the correlation is with resistance to receiving spiritual guidance as well.

3.

If the fingers move into the scalp beyond the hairline, the motion usually indicates the presence of a hidden and usually *terrible thought*, which impairs one's ability to deal with that issue or related issues. (See #7 in Forehead and Temple.)

No reckoning made...with all imperfections on my head.

- Shakespeare

*A belief
is
not true
because
it is
useful.*

- Amiel

4.
The hand to the side of the center of the head may refer to *a significant belief* that is limiting, destructive or causing difficulty in one's life, or to a conflict about believing or believing in someone or something.

5.
When both hands are placed on the head in this manner, the person is manifesting *disagreement between the sides* in areas of belief. This often is about "higher matters," including God.

6.
The hand lower on the side of the head above the ear usually refers to conflict about a person's *own identity and/or place* in the family and in society.

7.
Curiously, touching or scratching the "bump" on the side at the back of the head often indicates *an attitude* toward something as evil, or *an evil attitude* one may have. (Shades of phrenology!)

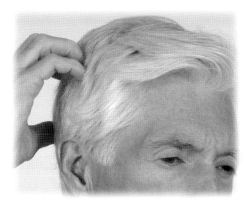

8.
The hand low on the back of the head along the occipital ridge usually indicates *trying to figure something out.*

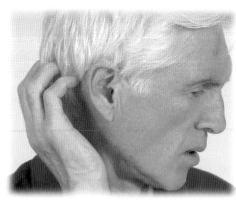

I do not understand; I pause; I examine.

- Montaigne

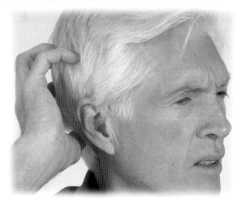

9.
The hand scratching at the back of the head indicates *puzzled or troubled* about something.

10.
When there is *recognition of the nature of the conflict* and one's position in regard to it, the hand will stop moving and the facial expression will usually reflect that perception.

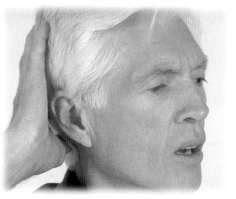

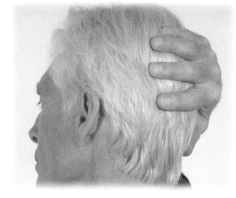

11.
If the hand holds a position on the back of the head, it usually indicates either a *position one is assuming now or a position taken in the past* on a similar matter.

*Stung by the splendour
of a sudden thought.*

- Robert Browning

*See what grace is
seated on this brow.*

- Shakespeare

The Forehead and Temple

It seems that many of the linguistic expressions about *the mind* refer to the brow, i.e., the forehead and temple area, coming from the age-old perception that our thinking is localized there. This is likely because we note how we repeatedly touch our brow in association with words that refer to mental activity, such as *idea, thought, notion*. Underlying the forehead are the frontal lobes, the part of the brain making us unique as humans and each human unique.

The size and shape of one's brow historically connotes one's level of intelligence. This is readily understood in the development of the size and slope of the forehead in proportion to the development of the frontal lobes. Early hominids had very little forehead or brow, for example. Thus, the terms *high brow* and *low brow* reflect both an evolutionary fact, but also the underlying attitude in society about an individual's level of development. It seems individuals tend to be judged by others, at least unconsciously, in this respect.

With foreheads villainous low.

- Shakespeare

Everyone seems to experience a hand to the forehead as comforting or reassuring, as mothers know so well when tending a sick child. Such a touch serves that purpose for all individuals at whatever age, whether it is with one's own hand or that of another, as noted in Chapter 1. A sense of unease or destabilization in oneself is likely caused by the desynchronization of the left and right brain hemispheres. When a person is experiencing conflict, a hand placed firmly on the forehead allows the person to feel a positive stabilizing effect, which can be demonstrated kinesiologically as well. In kinesiologic testing, when an individual's muscle strength diminishes in response to traumatic thoughts or memories or to telling a lie, a hand placed on the forehead will simultaneously allow a resumption of normal muscle strength as long as it is kept there, even while the person persists with the traumatic memory or with telling a lie. This is a useful exercise to try with someone experienced in kinesiology, should a person have doubts about the validity of what is being discussed here.

The troubled brow is referred to with expressions that suggest some aspect of disruptive thinking. A "furrowed brow" (horizontal lines) indicates worry, apprehension, or startle/surprise and, while it may be seen in most anyone, it is certainly more common in chronic anxiety. A "knit brow" (vertical lines), in which the eyebrows are temporarily pulled together so that a crease develops between them, indicates concentration with great intensity. When chronic, with resulting permanent crease lines, it indicates excessive pensiveness—thinking "too hard," "over-thinking." Not surprisingly, peptic ulceration is associated with a higher number of permanent vertical lines, as many as four.

When we say that a person has a "brow-beaten" expression, we are suggesting she looks as if she has been repeatedly harangued and has little response or defense. Other references to the forehead indicate care and emotion ("fevered brow"), age, the passage of time, and illness.

The lower limit of the brow is marked by the eyebrow, which is included (with the related symbolism) in Eye.

If every man's
internal care
Were written on
his brow,
How many
would
our pity share,
Who raise our
envy now.

- Walter Landor

General Attributes

*It would be
a good idea.*

- Gandhi

The forehead and temples are touched in reference to an idea, thought, notion, insight, or desire. It may refer to oneself, including the image one wishes to project, as well as to other people and things.

As in the photos of Albright and Marino on pages 10 and 11 and illustration #1 below, when the whole hand is placed firmly on the forehead, it is a powerful signal conveying the notion that the thought or memory is extremely disruptive and destabilizing. As a remedy, the hand is placed on the forehead in an attempt to regain one's balance.

A hand placed to the forehead as in #2 below is a more frequent personal motion and indicates a felt need to facilitate balancing the hemispheres. It may be done primarily to focus on difficult problem solving, requiring whole brain—especially frontal lobe—activity. This position often lasts longer than most self-referential touching.

*I balanced all,
brought all
to mind.*

- Yeats

Illustrations

1.
The classic response to an *overwhelming thought* is the hand put to the forehead. When a hand is placed on a troubled brow, as when a mother tends a sick child, it is comforting. So, too, when we do it for ourselves—the movement seems to steady or balance us; it is an attempt to unite the desynchronized (right and left) hemispheres.

2.

The hand, usually the edge, placed against the forehead, is a common motion that accompanies *reflection or attempts at problem solving,* and is an assist to hemispheric integration. The hand may even partially block visual sensory input to further facilitate cognitive focus.

Approach each new problem not with a view of finding what you hope will be there, but to get the truth.

- Bernard Baruch

3.

A hand to one side of the forehead refers to *recognition* of having forgotten something important, bad news, or a realization that one has made a major mistake. It may be a response to a *blocked thought* producing sudden discomfort. Such a *painful thought* might involve an unpleasant memory or not wanting to think a certain thought. If the forehead is slapped, there is a self-punitive aspect. This may also be gestural, that is, done deliberately to illustrate one's feelings.

I have a pain in my forehead, here.

- Shakespeare

4.

A hand to the frontal vertical area usually refers to a *one's desired image*, i.e., how *one wants to be seen*. It is interesting to note that a distinctive marking in this area on animals, such as dogs and horses, is known as a blaze and provides a form of singular identification. (See #5 in Eye.)

It matters not what you are seen to be, but what you are.

- Publilius Syrus

5.

A finger to the temple indicates a response to *an idea or thought charged* with unexpressed emotion. The idea or thought may prove hard to change, persisting and repeating, leading to obsessive type thinking. Often a person will be unable to reason himself out of it until and unless the emotion is expressed.

6.

A finger to the superior temporal area generally indicates a sense of *can't get to something*, as if it is more elusive than the reference above. The finger generally is stroking that area, rubbing up and down.

7.

Touching the upper frontal area indicates *a thought* that has an intended result or wished-for result. Generally the touch is with more than one finger. (See #3 in Head.)

8.

A finger on the hairline of the forehead indicates *a thought that moves from the seen to the unseen*, as in not wanting others—or even oneself—to be aware of the content. It often relates to manifestations of dominance or power which, if disclosed, would diminish them. The finger often runs briefly along the hairline.

Thoughts unexpressed may sometimes fall back dead.

- Will Carleton

9.

A finger on the hairline, touching the back of the temple area, indicates *a notion*, i.e., a *movement in the general direction of knowing*—at the same time encountering a block on the side that is touched. This is usually discovered to be a *fixation* in regard to that topic, with a necessity to avoid something which at an earlier time caused the person great pain.

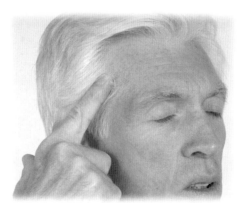

Pluck from memory a rooted sorrow.

- Shakespeare

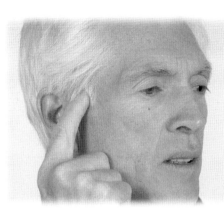

10.
A finger in front of the ear in the posterior temple area indicates *a desire* that is particularly strong on one side. For example, a desire to be with people may not be shared equally with the other side, or is even resisted by the other side (an internal quarrel).

Quarrels would not last long if the fault were only on one side.

- La Rochefoucauld

11.
When the fingers start low on both temples and stroke upward, at times repeatedly, the movement seems to indicate *frustration of thought processes or frustration about fully elaborating* an idea, i.e., *getting both sides together*. As in photo #6, the movement represents the inability to "get to something," but indicates a joint effort (both brains) to do so.

Both worlds at once they view.

- Edmund Waller

12.
When the fingers stop at both temples, it appears to indicate a sense of resolution of the conflict, i.e., *an idea that is satisfying* or at least *acceptable to both sides.*

Even a single hair casts its shadow.

\- Publilius Syrus

The Hair

Darwinian Man,
though
well-behaved,
at best is only a
monkey shaved.

- W.S. Gilbert

The hair evokes fascination for many reasons, including the virtue of the thinness of a single hair, the countless number of hairs, the rapid and continuing growth, the varying colors among individuals and within the same individual over time and, of course, the effect it has on one's appearance. The hair on our heads, body hair, and male facial hair are all vestiges of our evolutionary past. The title of Desmond Morris's popular book *The Naked Ape* humorously implies this conflict between the civilized human and the "beastly" part of us, reflected in the persisting vestiges of hairiness inherited from our mammalian ancestors.

The only place we humans have plentiful hair is on our heads—with some exceptions, of course. Women generally tend to remove hair from parts of the body where it is unwanted, depending on the norms of the culture, although men have more cultural leeway with facial hair. Porphyria is a rare disorder in individuals that results in an overabundance of facial hair; at the end of the 19th and into the 20th centuries, people who suffered from this abnormality sometimes traveled as oddities in circus side shows.

As has been verified by research in recent years, an individual's blood pressure lowers when petting or stroking the fur of an animal. Perhaps this physical response also comes to us from our evolutionary past; grooming in apes, monkeys, and other mammals—one individual inspecting, cleaning, stroking the fur of another—appears to result in the groomer getting as much comfort and reassurance as the groomee. This interpersonal contact manifested by physical touching facilitates and often results in bonding between individuals, no matter the species.

In the same way, when a mother strokes the head of her child the action shows affection for the child and probably has a soothing physical benefit for the mother as well. It is likely that stroking one's own hair may also produce a physiologically calming effect, and that a man strokes his beard or moustache at times for just the same reason.

As an element of the body that is most easily and obviously altered, the hair gets generous attention in most cultures, particularly from women—a woman's hair is referred to as her "crowning glory." In many cultures today, as it has been for centuries, women cover their hair in church because of its associated sexual attractiveness.

Classically, hair has been associated with power. One thinks of Samson whose long hair symbolized and contained his power. Beards and moustaches generally are seen as expressions of attaining manhood, and various religious leaders grow beards to signify their wisdom and status. However, the power of a woman's hair, in all its symbolic manifestations, has eclipsed that of a man's, except perhaps for Samson's—but it was a woman who ultimately took his power from him.

Fear causes the muscle attached to the hair follicle to contract, as do cold temperatures, and this is referred to as pilo-erection. A dangerous situation, then, may be "hair raising," and extreme fear may cause a person's hair to "stand on end." Anxiety is manifested by the expression suggesting a precarious situation, "hanging by a hair." Another emotion commonly associated with hair is frustration which, when marked, will cause an individual to "tear her hair out." When something is bothersome, an effort to get rid of it, "get it out of my hair," will be made.

One hair of a woman can draw more than a hundred pair of oxen.

- James Howell

The very hair on my head stand up for dread.

- Sophocles

General Attributes

Playing with the hair, such as twisting or lightly pulling the hair, seems to occur when one is troubled—feeling fearful or unsettled, for example. If these actions are performed out of habit as a residue of self-comforting adaptive behavior from our early years, then they do not have the specificity of personal body language.

Grooming motions have sexual and power implications and are easily distinguishable from playing with the hair. Context and facial expression are helpful aids in making the distinction.

Grabbing or pulling hard on one's own hair (sometimes causing discomfort or even pain) reflects sheer frustration and possibly self-abuse.

She smoothes her hair with automatic hand.

- T.S. Eliot

Illustration

1.
Stroking or grooming motions that occur with the hair refer to wanting to appear attractive, having to do with *sexual and/or power* implications.

A similar motion—running the hand through the hair but contacting the scalp—has a different implication, that of attempting to stimulate mental activity when conflict is dulling receptivity. (See Head.)

God has given you one face,
*   And you make yourselves another.*

-Shakespeare

The Face

The face is the most distinguishing part of the body by far, and the principal means of nonverbal communication is through facial expression.

Notes Paul Ekman:

> *The human face—in repose and in movement, at the moment of death as in life, in silence and in speech, when seen or sensed from within, in actuality or as represented in art or recorded by the camera—is a commanding, complicated, and at times confusing source of information. The face is commanding because of its very visibility and omnipresence....The complexity of the face is apparent when we consider its sending capacity, the information it may convey, and its role in social life* (1972, p.1).

But to prepare a face to meet the faces that you meet.

- T.S. Eliot

We present our face to the world. It is the principal aspect of our identity and is the outstanding feature by which we recognize others. The face is also the primary display unit in social context and as such it communicates whether we intend it to or not. Our facial displays influence our social relationships and, in turn, the culture in which we live shapes our facial displays.

Aware of the potential to communicate thoughts that perhaps expose oneself or are not congruent with the situation, we have learned to deal with face-to-face encounters with socially appropriate facial expressions, whether in a business setting or in our personal lives. In the security of our intimate relationships we are perhaps less vigilant about what our faces are saying and not so conscious of controlling our expressions—the private face versus the public face.

Characteristics of the face change over time, both as a consequence of aging and in response to interaction with the world. Responding to his secretary's surprise when he indicated he did not like a certain man's face, Abraham Lincoln said, "After 40 every man is responsible for his face." He recognized that our attitudes, feelings, and reactions to others and events in our lives help to shape our faces. Individuals living together for many years may often come to resemble each other, which may be attributed to like attitudes and reactions that cause development of similar expression lines. The face reflects both inherent and acquired characteristics, and each half of the face seems to reflect and manifest the activity of the associated brain hemisphere. (See Chapter 5.)

Many expressions indicate the symbolism of *face.* "On the face of it" refers to outward appearances and what things seem. When we are hiding our feelings, we are "putting on a good face." A "long face" calls up the idea of sadness.

Being able to "face it" suggests strength in the "face" of adversity, and one "faces up" to a problem by admitting it. Putting both hands to the face, hiding it, a person "buries his face," indicating feeling overwhelmed or ashamed.

Effects on self-esteem and personal or familial integrity are indicated by the expressions "losing face" and "saving face." A parent might say to a child, "Don't show me that face"—a phrase that could, if used frequently, prove detrimental to the child's self-esteem.

We may go "face to face" in a debate and "face down" a foe. We show opposition by "setting one's face against" someone or something. Putting in an appearance, an individual "shows his face." Duplicity is indicated when referring to someone as "two-faced."

There's no art to find the mind's construction in the face.

- Shakespeare

And how am I to face the odds Of man's bedevilment and God's?

- A.E. Housman

There are many references to colors seen in the face and most deal with emotion. An individual may be "red in the face" in embarrassment, "green with envy," "purple with rage," "white as a ghost" with fear.

The most common responses in Kinoetics are those of the hand touching specific features of the face, with symbolism related to each part. Thus, the parts of the face are addressed individually in the following sections.

*The face
is the mirror
of the mind.*

- St. Jerome

General Attributes

When the entire face is covered or rubbed, the conflict symbolized appears to be about "facing up to it" (or not). The response usually refers to feeling overwhelmed and/or wishing to avoid what is feared. A variation on the symbolism of covering one's face with the hands suggests "hiding one's face"—the head is usually tilted downward ("face down"), an indication of shame.

Illustration

1.
When the hands cover the face, the reference is usually to feeling *overwhelmed with resulting avoidance,* motivated by fear and consequently not being able to "face it." As this response is an action that hides the face, it may also relate to *shame.*

Rubbing the face vigorously may be preparatory to *getting ready to face it,* and/or may be thought of as trying to remove the barriers to the difficulties of "facing up." It is a stimulating motion similar to running one's hand over the top of the head.

There's language in her eye.

- Shakespeare

The Eye

In the East where faces are read with a goal of evaluating an individual's abilities and liabilities, eyes are thought to reflect both intelligence and the energy available within. In the West our literature suggests they are more the "mirror of the soul," but in a similar way are believed to express a depth of feeling and vitality—or lack of it—more that any other physical feature. Traditionally, the expression of feeling through the eyes is seen as a powerful mode of communication, and the corollary of this is that eye contact reflects both levels of self-confidence and/or honesty. Most individuals feel they have a certain facility for judging others on the basis of their eyes, yet it is not usually possible to pinpoint the qualities of the eyes that are the basis for these evaluations.

*The light
of the body
is in the eye.*

- The Bible: Matthew

We do sense that truthfulness, perhaps more than any other quality, is communicated with the eye. This is not simply the state of being truthful or not, as a mother might ask her child to "look me in the eye and tell me…." Perhaps a more generic honesty can be seen in the eye relating to the aspect of truth we call integrity, including the courage to see whatever there is to be seen, however personally challenging. Essentially, the eye perceives light, and the metaphorical use of the concept of light as the equivalent of fully knowing, of ultimate truth, is present in religious traditions throughout the world.

Symbolism in reference to the eye is varied and not only involves seeing but also the reaction to what is seen. On the alert, a person keeps "her eyes wide open," "a watchful eye" or "an eye out" or has "eyes in the back of her head." Sly vigilance is noted when a person observes her surroundings "out of the corner of her eye." And an individual takes care of business when "seeing after" (something).

The importance of the eye as a major feature in giving and getting attention is indicated by "catching her eye," "getting the eye/giving the eye." A person who is lovesick has "stars in her eyes" and "eyes only" for the focus of her attention.

Profound appreciation is expressed by "feasting our eyes on," and composure is reflected in the phrase "not batting an eye." We demonstrate honesty or forthrightness by "looking a person in the eye."

All things flourish where you turn your eyes.

- Alexander Pope

General Attributes

The significance of touching the eyes refers to conflict about where or even whether to direct one's attention or awareness. It refers to what is seen or unseen, or what one wishes to avoid seeing. Associated rubbing of the eyes clearly relates to sadness.

Other signs referencing the eyes indicate a person's view or perception— including one's view of self, i.e., self-image—as well as the restriction of view and the limits of an individual's awareness or belief. The significance of touching the eyes or surrounding areas is also related to whether they are open or closed.

Illustrations

1.
One of the most common signs of conflict is that of rubbing one eye with the forefinger or hand. The reference is to *not wanting to see*, associated with *sadness*, as if "it's too much" and "it would make me too sad to see." This response often relates to a trauma experienced at a young age or a present experience that associates to that early trauma.

*Eyes they have,
but they see not.*

- The Bible: Psalms

2.
Rubbing both eyes, indicating *not wanting to see and sadness*, suggests it is going to be quite hard for the person to deal with the issue as both sides (male and female) are involved. A motion on both sides of the body simultaneously suggests a doubly important or difficult challenge—so that both sides feel impaired or limited.

3.

This important movement indicates *not wanting to see*, as in rubbing the eye or eyes (above), but *without the associated sadness*. (See the photo opposite. What might Newt Gingrich not want to see?)

4.

This response is quite different from the photo above and actually seems opposite in meaning. The reference is to *now seeing* something that wasn't apparent before, by "clearing away the debris," as if picking a "sleepy seed" out of the eye in the morning. Note that the finger is facing in the opposite direction to #3 above.

5.

A finger placed between the eyes on the bridge of the nose (polarity point) seems to refer to one's *self-image*. As the midpoint between the eyes, the location likely denotes the composite picture of the right and left brain.

If only we face the facts, as they say, with both eyes open.

- Copernicus

The area of the Hindu "third eye" is just above the point shown in #5. A finger placed here seems to refer to an attempt to gain insight or resolve conflict.

After the 1998 mid-term elections and the controversy surrounding his leadership and conduct, Newt Gingrich meets the press and announces that he is stepping down as Speaker of the House. He seems to be indicating that there is something he does not want to see or feel.

(Kennerly/Corbis Sygma)

These two following photos have been placed in this section on Eye to facilitate understanding the symbolism. They are just as appropriately placed in Forehead and Temple, as they indicate seeing by the "angle" of viewing and the "lenses" of perception.

6.
Touching the eyebrow refers to *one's view* on a subject. When the eyebrows move up and down, the movement emphasizes the expression in the eyes and *one's attitude.* The responses shown here and below are often done in a stroking manner.

We can easily represent things as we wish them to be.

- Aesop

7.
When the finger is placed above the eyebrow, the reference seems to be to something broader than one's view, i.e., that of one's *perception,* which consists of one's beliefs and assumptions.

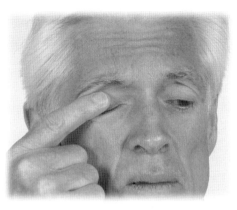

8.
When the upper eyelid is stroked or rubbed deliberately, it indicates *a sad view*.

*"I think till
I'm weary of
thinking,"
Said the sad-eyed
Hindu King,
"And I see
but shadows
around me."*

- Sir Alfred Lyall

9.
When the finger strokes between the upper eyelid and the eyebrow, the reference is to a *limiting point of view*.

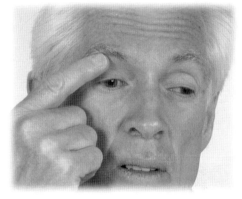

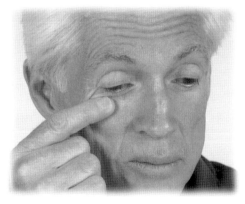

10.
The finger discreetly wiping underneath the eye suggests wiping away a tear, and represents a more *adult form of sadness or grief* than rubbing the whole eye with the hand, as a child is more apt to do.

11.
When the finger is placed to the outside corner of the eye, the motion seems to indicate that there is something *beyond one's vision or belief*, i.e., something that is quite peripheral and would require a willingness to redirect one's vision in order to see it.

12.
As the finger stretches the eye, the suggestion is that one is being stretched *beyond the limit of one's vision or belief.*

It is only with the heart that one can see rightly; what is essential is invisible to the eye.

- St. Exupery

13.
When stretching the eyes with both fingers, the reference seems to be that this matter is *beyond belief, out of sight, or beyond one's capacity to see*, as both sides are involved.

*I shut my eyes
in order to see.*

- Paul Gauguin

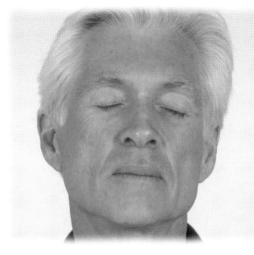

14.
A person may shut the eyes to momentarily stop seeing as a symbolic way to *reduce the sense of conflict* or even *avoid conflict*. The motion may not be conflict related but may indicate an effort to *facilitate remembering* because imagery becomes clearer with the eyes closed. It may also represent an attempt to avoid distraction in order to bring other faculties of the mind into play.

15.
While closing the eyes may or may not indicate conflict, closing the eyes *tightly*, a common facial expression in little children signifying *not wanting to see*, appears to have the same significance for adults—there is something he *won't let himself see.*

*Whosoever shall smite thee
on thy right cheek,
turn to him the other also.*

\- The Bible: Matthew

The Cheek

Cheeks can be seen as useful signals in society. Studies show that along with a baby's large eyes and high rounded forehead, a baby's plump cheeks are attractive in a way that inspires parental love and attention. When we blush from embarrassment or turn pale with illness, our cheeks reflect our emotional or physical state. If someone is tired or sick, her "cheeks are drawn," but when a person is in good health, her cheek is "ruddy," rosy, round.

When a couple is "cheek to cheek," intimacy is inferred. The cheek presents itself for affection—for touches or kisses that can be intimate or purely social. Conversely, the cheek may receive a slap in a display of insult or combativeness—historically, a challenge to a duel. An individual who is bold or impudent might be referred to as "cheeky," as if offering the cheek to invite physical confrontation.

"Turning the cheek" has cultural and religious significance implying forgiveness or forebearance, the phrase appearing in various forms in the Bible.

General Attributes

Touching the cheek signifies a person or situation that is associated with either affection or insult/injury, or both.

The hand drawn down the cheek, especially both hands, signifies fatigue with a situation or a loss of ability to cope with difficulties.

*Care
Sat on her
faded cheek.*

- John Milton

Illustrations

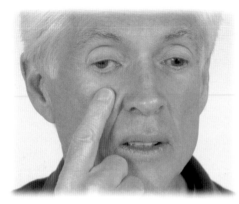

1.
The finger below the middle of the eye often indicates *needy* and usually refers to a person, particularly parents and often God. The finger starts higher and pulls down slightly. This is the first point on the stomach meridian acupuncture point; *needy* is an emotion that relates to blocked energy in the stomach meridian.

2.
Touching the cheekbone (zygoma) often seems to signify a *conflict about change*; this position indicates *a situation*, e.g., one's financial situation, which in turn may be about one's relationship to money, beliefs about money, resultant motives, etc.

3.
But further back the position seems to refer to a *conflict about change* in relationship to *a person*, or even a group, including one's own culture and country.

We do not succeed in changing things according to our desire, but gradually our desire changes. The situation that we hoped to change because it was intolerable becomes unimportant.

- Proust

4.
Hands on both cheeks, extending up from the neck, suggest *discouragement*, i.e., "hope draining away."

Forlorn!
the very word
is a bell
To toll me back...
to my sole self.

\- John Keats

5.
In a more extreme movement, the hands pull the face and lower lids down, indicating *forlorn*.

Oon ere it herde, at tothir out it went.
(In one ear and out the other.)

- Chaucer

The Ear

The ear is marvelously designed for hearing because it is cupped in such a way as to amplify and direct sound to the eardrum. Each ear is highly distinctive in its external shape, an individuality analogous to a fingerprint. Darwin thought the bump on the edge of the ear, carried by a sizeable percentage of the population, is vestigial and indicates that we come from a lineage in which ears were pointed. The same inference might be drawn from noting that a small number of people can wiggle their ears as can many of our mammalian cousins.

We respond to sound or show attention to someone by "giving an ear," "lending an ear," "pricking up our ears." Hyper-alertness is indicated by being "all ears" or "having an ear to the ground." A person may turn a "deaf ear" to ignore someone, but a thought or idea cannot be ignored when someone has a "bug in his ear."

Emotions can be felt in the ear—shame or anger makes the "ears burn." Excessive or unnecessary speech amounts to "talking his ears off." A catastrophic life event is indicated by the phrase "the world came crashing down around his ears."

*This flea which
I have
in mine ear.*

- Rabelais

*They have ears,
but they
hear not.*

- The Bible: Psalms

General Attributes

Touching the ear references conflict about attending to what is heard, overheard, wishes to hear, or fears hearing. The motion may indicate difficulty processing what is heard, or even signal selective hearing, refusal to hear, or not hearing.

A finger placed behind the ear seems to signify rebelliousness or protest, whereas a finger placed in front of the ear seems to signify desire. Perhaps these positions refer to liking or not liking what we are hearing or have heard.

The earlobe is an appendix to the ear and does not facilitate hearing. When touched, it may be as if fingering an earring (a motion made by both women and men) and seems to be in reference to the material world, i.e., not only jewelry but wealth, money, and even status.

If the lobe is pulled on, however, the movement most often seems to refer to falsehood or a debate about how much truthfulness a person is willing to manifest, or even to outright lying.

Remember, there's always a voice saying the right thing to you somewhere if you'll only listen for it.

- Thomas Hayes

Illustrations

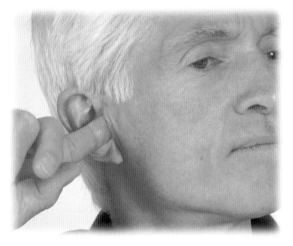

1.
A finger **in** the ear canal suggests an *unwillingness to hear the topic* under discussion, at least on that side (masculine or feminine side). Children will often put fingers in both ears and the meaning of that action is quite clear.

2.
The finger **above** the ear canal inside the ear seems to refer to *having heard more* than was intended from another person, including *over-hearing* something said that was meant to be kept private. The symbolism of the finger over the ear canal seems obvious.

He that hath ears to hear, let him hear.

- The Bible: Mark

3.
The finger **below** the ear canal and inside the ear seems to indicate *fear of hearing.*

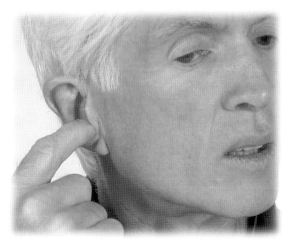

4.
The finger directly in front of the ear may refer to *a desire to hear* (that one is loved, appreciated, or welcomed). Touching the foremost soft tissue of the ear, behind the position of the finger shown here, seems to indicate *wishing to hear* something other than what was just said.

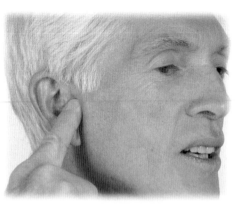

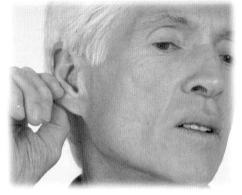

5.
Fingering the back of the ear seems to indicate having heard *mixed messages*, that is, contradictory messages.

The words of truth are always paradoxical.

- Lao Tzu

6.
Touching farther up the ear, particularly when pulling, often refers to something *hidden or secret*.

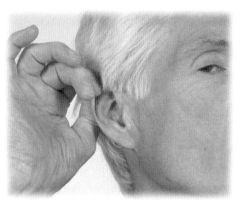

7.
Fingering the earlobe, as if playing with jewelry, although somewhat more common in women, occurs in men as well. The motion refers to the *material world,* that is, money, home, things, status.

I do not mind lying, But I hate inaccuracy.

- Samuel Butler

8.
Pulling on the earlobe is analogous to "pulling one's leg." This motion indicates an individual is *contemplating lying, is actually lying, or has lied.* It is as if, hearing his own lie, the person is attempting to disown what he has said, perhaps "pulling" the lie away from the ear. (The term *leakage* has particularly been applied in reference to body movements that inadvertently signal lying.)

9.

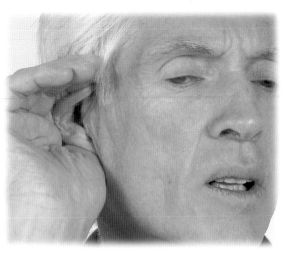

This illustration is an example of the critical importance of context. The motion is common with the hard of hearing who use it as an assist to extend the ear to amplify sound. As a gesture, this obvious signal indicates that someone should speak up. But as a Kinoetic response, it refers to a conflict about a person *wanting to hear more* about what is said, or refers to what *that side wants to hear now, or wanted to hear.*

*I was all ear
And took in
strains that
might create
a soul.*

- John Milton

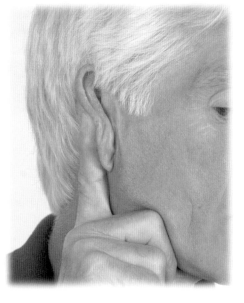

10.

A distinctive position is the placement of the finger in back of the ear, which is pushed slightly forward. The motions are exaggerated here and in the photo above; the ear in this example is not usually fully closed. The reference is to *selective hearing,* suggesting there are some things a person is *unwilling to hear.*

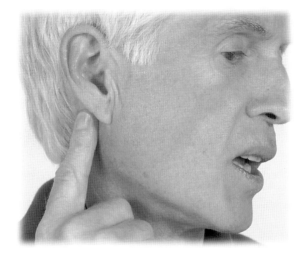

11.
A finger on the mastoid process, the bump directly behind the ear, seems to refer to a *rebellious attitude*, often associated *with guilt.*

*Guilt has
very quick ears
to an accusation.*

- Henry Fielding

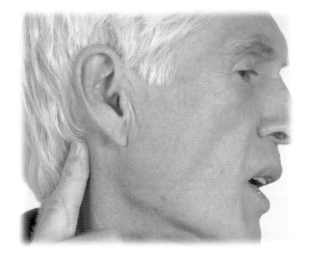

12.
A finger posterior to the mastoid process seems to signify an attitude of *protest,* usually *without guilt.*

It takes little talent to see clearly
what lies under one's nose,
a good deal of it to know
in which direction
to point that organ.

\- W.H. Auden

The Nose

In personal body language, the most common touch to the face is that to the nose. Perhaps this is because "the nose knows"—an old folk expression and one made better known by Dr. Milton Erickson.

As a nose on a man's face,
Or a weathercock on a steeple.

- Shakespeare

The neurophysiologic explanation for the particular importance of the nose as related to emotion involves the direct connection to the limbic system, the seat of emotion within the brain. In animals, the importance of the nose is obvious, and, although the human sense of smell is greatly diminished from that of our presumed ancestors, the connections to the limbic system are still along the ancient pathways that relate to our basic instincts and drives.

Observing how many creatures in the family of mammals use their noses to pursue their needs and wants, we may apply this knowledge to humans and the symbolic references to touching the nose in relation to those large topics of survival, sex, and aggression.

If a person is determined and aggressive in pursuing goals, we say that he is "hard-nosed"; he may be so single-minded or self-preoccupied that he "can't see past the nose on his face." If an individual satisfies some whim or emotion at the expense of more important needs, he is "cutting off his nose to spite his face," that is, engaging in self-defeating behavior. When one's "nose is out of joint," resentment or irritability is indicated. "Paying through the nose" refers to paying an excessive price (in money, emotion, time, etc.) for something. Like a hound, a detective follows his instincts to "sniff out clues"—he is "nosing around." If someone gets in the way of another person's aggressive needs, the result may be an "itchy nose" indicating "itching for a fight."

General Attributes

The connection of the nose to the limbic system, the emotional brain, is directed toward getting what we need or want, or getting rid of what is not needed or wanted.

Thus, much of the touching of the nose results from conflict related to the function of valuation, and then either to approach or avoidance, or to a continued conflict about what to do if one is ambivalent.

Other hand movements to the nose may indicate an awareness that something is not quite clear or clarification is sought. ("You can see it and I can't, but I am getting there.") Touching the end of the nose, particularly pushing or scratching, seems to indicate that a person is getting in touch with something important that is "as plain as the nose on my face"—but still can't see it.

Touching either side of the bridge of the nose seems to relate to the pituitary points indicative of denial, as not thinking or not feeling.

Illustrations

1.
In this important motion, a finger to the side of the bridge of the nose (the pituitary field, i.e., the "master gland") indicates *an unwillingness to think or feel*, leading to *denial*, and blocking a person's integrity and responsibility for himself.

One who never feels
The wanton stings and motions of the senses.

- Shakespeare

*If I am
not for myself,
who is for me?
And if I am
only for myself,
what am I?*

- Hillel

2.
A finger placed further down the middle of the nose seems to refer to *values*, including how a person values himself.

3.
One hand holding the nose suggests *studying the matter* at hand as if with great thought or concern to know how the matter being considered fits into one's own value system.

4.
Stroking the nose downward, possibly in a repeated motion, may be done as one is *attempting to reach a decision* (coaxing it out of the nose, so to speak). "The nose knows."

5.
A finger placed alongside the nose,
usually stroking downward,
indicates *unexpressed sadness*.
(The tear never shed.)

'Tis what I feel
but can't define,
'Tis what I know
but can't express.

- Beilby Porteus

6.
This common motion of a finger
positioned along the wing of the
nose or with a quick stroke
is a common sign of conflict,
representing *disagreement*. It often
indicates internal disagreement
within a person, but may also
represent external disagreement,
including *deception* or even
non-compliance in response
to the disagreement.

7.
Touching both sides of the nose, usually with a brief stroking motion, seems to indicate *both sides disagreeing* and thus there is a *double bind*; that is, both sides of an individual are in conflict with *no way out*.

I begin to smell a rat.

- Shakeseare

8.
The fingers here squeeze or pinch the nose then briefly hold it (as distinguished from above) as a way to signal a bad smell, "something stinks." It usually refers to an external stimulus, such as *what someone is doing, wants to do, or have someone else do.*

9.

Pushing on the end of the nose seems to mean "looky here," as in: "You can see it and I can't so *help me see* what is clearer to you than it is to me"—the person is unconsciously asking for help.

Whereas...

As plain as a nose in a man's face.

- Rabelais

10.

... scratching the end of the nose seems to be an individual's own attempt to *get in touch with the issue*, that is, doing it for himself.

11.
The fingertip placed under the nose, where it may rest or push the nose upward, suggests *snobbery;* that is, "my position is superior." Curiously, it may also be an attempt to be more receptive. The tone of voice and topic of discussion usually help clarify the meaning.

Snobbery is the pride of those who are not sure of their position.

- Berton Braley

12.
The fingertip flicking the underside of the nose indicates some degree of *contemptuous behavior,* even to the degree of *despising.* Ironically, it may refer to *snubbing someone for snobbery.*

13.

A finger placed under the nose in a stationary manner seems to have to do with *hesitancy or restraint* (as if to hold back a sneeze).

14.

A common motion is that of the finger stroking the underside of the nose in one swipe. This generally is a *dismissive* movement or at least a *deprecatory* one. It can indicate *a wish to get rid of or be rid of something.* ("That's it.") It is often accompanied by a sniff or snort which may be barely audible.

15.

Rubbing back and forth under the nose seems to indicate *not wanting to betray one's feelings* (e.g., hurt or sad); thus, it is an attempt to "be brave," as a child wiping a runny nose. It may even suggest a willingness to fight if pushed.

If I truly showed my feelings, the other guys would eat me alive.

- Michael McGill

16.
Rubbing the nose more vigorously seems to indicate *irritation* with a situation. It is sometimes followed by a sneeze.

Those who in quarrels interpose Must often wipe a bloody nose.

- John Gay

17.
In one instance, the finger inside the nostril is a *hostile gesture* meaning "screw you," usually accompanied by a congruent facial expression or by flicking the finger out of the nose.

18.
The finger inside the nostril may also indicate a *desire for sexuality*, usually with an *aggressive connotation*, with more of a hostile tone than a loving one.

*Not that which goeth into the mouth
defileth a man;
but that which cometh out of the mouth,
this defileth a man.*

- The Bible: Matthew

The Mouth

From birth, the primary duty of the mouth is to ensure our survival not only by taking in food and water but by allowing us to signal our basic needs.

His heart's his mouth What his breast forges, that his tongue must vent.

- Shakespeare

The mouth and lips allow us to express ourselves through sounds and language, which have direct (denotative) and symbolic (connotative) value. In this sense, *the mouth is where the heart and brain/mind meet*. The mouth also speaks in many ways in addition to articulating words, whether with smiles or frowns, puckered lips or protruding tongue.

The lips are mobile, highly expressive, and intensely sensitive with their dense concentration of nerve endings. This sensitivity, associated with the expressiveness and mobility of the mouth, lends to the obvious association with sexuality. We kiss with the lips, women color their lips to enhance their appeal. Poets and romantics have long written about the virtual and symbolic connection between love and lips, so it is interesting that negative connotations should be associated with the lips. What of the curious expression "kiss off," signifying rejection? This phrase perhaps comes from the Biblical account of Judas whose disrespect and betrayal of Jesus was paradoxically signified with a kiss. The phrase "giving one lip" shows disrespect combined with combativeness.

Many symbolic references to the mouth, lips, and tongue in popular usage relate to revealing oneself, sometimes inadvertently, and expressing emotion in various ways. Referring to an individual as a "loud mouth" or "big mouth" suggests egocentricity, including braggadocio. When a person is "shooting off his mouth" or "running off at the mouth," he is being indiscreet. "Laughing out of the side of his mouth" is an expression indicating facetiousness, often with arrogance. Thoughtlessness or a hidden motive may be exposed by a "slip of the tongue." Difficulty expressing oneself results in being told to "spit it out."

The teeth seem the most symbolically primal of our features, as they relate to our animal cousins who use their teeth to grip and hold, rip and tear, and remain a clue to mankind's aggressive history. When a person "sinks his teeth" into a job, he is fully and aggressively engaged with it. When someone is "armed to the teeth," he is ready for combat.

My heart was in my mouth.

- Petronius

General Attributes

Touching the lips or surrounding area signifies conflict concerning what to say, knowing enough to say it, or even whether to say it, resulting in hesitancy. The movement also may reflect the perceived status of one's position relative to the matter being considered, i.e., whether one feels superior to, equal to, or inferior to the person or task or subject matter being considered and/or addressed.

Touching (often with a stroking motion) the lines of expression around the mouth relates to conflict about just that—expressing oneself.

I was trying to make my mouth say I would do the right thing and the clean thing.

- Mark Twain

Touching one's teeth seems to have to do with conflict about "getting into it" (the fray, the fracas, the challenge), that is, conflict about too much or too little aggressiveness. Touching the incisors relates to "cutting into" (incisive, incision). A specific and important motion is that of placing the fingernail between the two front teeth, symbolizing a block/barrier to integration of the right and left brain hemispheres.

Illustrations

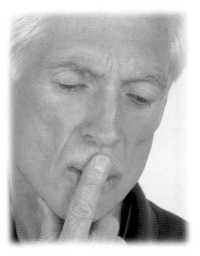

1.
The finger touching the midline above the lips but **pressed** against the lips, as if to say "shhhhh," seems to signify that *one shouldn't say anything*— "button your lip." Variations include the finger(s) curled over the lips, and placement of other fingers and the thumb on significant chin points. (This also applies to #2.)

2.
The finger **over** the lips touching the nose at the midline indicates, *"I must not talk until I know more."*

Take care and say this with presence of mind.

- Terence

3.
The finger **touching** the midline between nose and lips seems to relate to *both sides trying to unite, to agree, to bridge the gap*. At the same time, the motion refers to the presence of an obstacle that prevents agreement. The obstacle is often the lack of respect for the ability, i.e., the value of the other side. The fingertip is in contact with the midline above the lips, and the finger is often bent and does not touch the lips. (In the developing embryo, this cleavage the last to close—if it does not, the result is the defect called a cleft or "hare" lip.)

4.

The finger touching either of the lines of expression that run from the nose around the mouth indicates a *difficulty in expressing oneself.* The motion is often made with precision, as if drawing the expression line itself. A young face has faint or no lines of expression; lines develop with age and deepen in relation to how facially expressive a person has been.

5.

The finger to the side of the line of expression seems to indicate conflict about *expressing feeling, or feelings about expressing oneself,* and whether or not one feels free to do so.

"Then you should say what you mean," the March Hare went on. *"I do,"* Alice...replied; *"at least... I mean what I say."*

- Lewis Carroll

6.

Biting the lower lip seems to indicate *restraint and uncertainty about trusting,* including the *ability to trust oneself,* i.e., self-doubt. The motion manifests on the conflicted side.

7.
Touching the lower lip with one finger more directly points to an issue of *feeling inferior* and may also reflect the relationship between inferiority and lack of confidence.

Those men who become famous more through their infinite inferiority.

- Herman Melville

8.
Touching the lower lip with two fingers, one on each side of the midline, usually symbolizes the same as #7 above, but involves *both sides* of the personality.

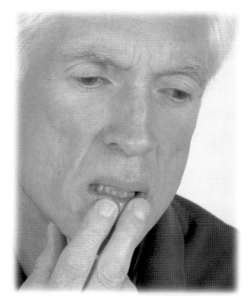

9.
The finger **above** the upper lip seems to reflect *superiority*, just as touching the lower lip indicates inferiority.

O! What a deal of scorn looks beautiful In the contempt and anger of his lip.

- Shakespeare

10.
The finger at the **edge** of the upper lip seems to indicate the way *one feels about another person,* i.e., one's position compared to that of another.

11.
The finger **on** the upper lip would seem to refer to *the question of equality.* If it occurs in the process of agreeing with someone to *seem to be equal,* it more often signifies *hyprocrisy.*

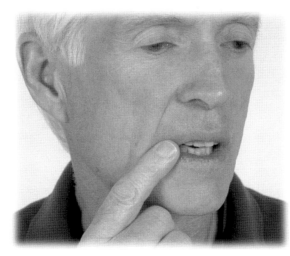

12.
The finger to the corner of the mouth seems to reflect that one is *thinking about what to say.*

And love,
grown faint
and fearful
With lips
but half regretful.

- Swinburne

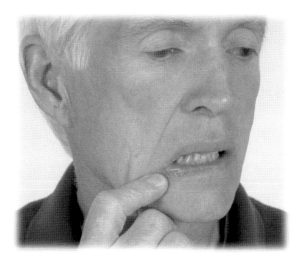

13.
When one corner of the mouth is pulled down, it may refer to *something that was said*, generally something *unpleasant or ill conceived*, as if something "slipped out." The sense is, "I wish I hadn't said that."

14.
Covering the mouth may indicate *debating what to say,* perhaps due to the uncertainly about how speaking one's mind would be received; the debate involves the need to say and the likely unpleasant consequences.

Out of thine own mouth will I judge thee.

- The Bible: Luke

15.
Covering the mouth and pulling the sides together seems to indicate *deliberation, as if trying to get the two sides to agree* about how to say something (as if trying to "get it all together").

New York Mayor Rudolph Giuliani pauses during a press conference as he speaks about the shooting death of a man by city police. Forty-one shots were reported to have hit the unarmed man. Mayor Giuliani indicates the need to restrain himself from saying the wrong thing in a tense situation.

(AP/Wide World Photos)

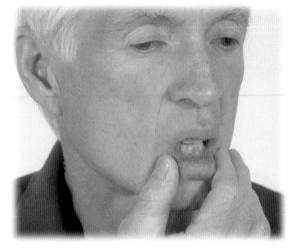

16.
The symbolism of this motion is similar to #13 but involves both sides. It usually refers to a disagreement about *which side would have said it better or might have said it differently.*

*Our eyes
are what one is,
one's mouth
is what one
becomes.*

- John Galsworthy

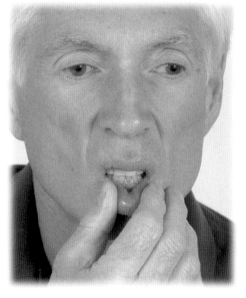

17.
When the fingers pull together, squeezing the lower lip, the symbolism seems to represent the effort of one side to obtain help from the other side to *pull the sides together to speak the whole truth.* The resistant side is being coaxed to speak in agreement—whether or not agreement has been reached. ("He/she wants me to give or say something that I don't want to.")

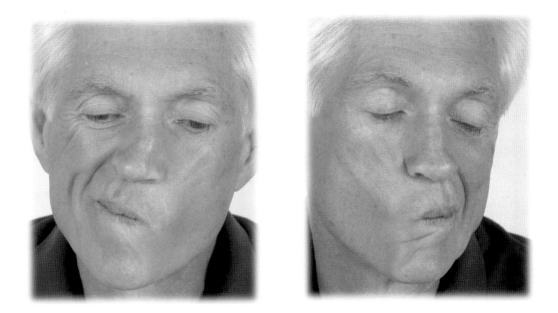

18.
This movement generally refers to one side *disowning* an idea being entertained by the other, and is "blaming" *the other side for being solely responsible for the thought or feeling.* The disowning side is actually pushing, rather than the "bunched up" side pulling.

In the great majority of individuals, the left side (the right brain hemisphere) manifests this pushing motion in reaction to feeling *consistently overridden* by the dominant left hemisphere, thus supporting Shakespeare's observation:

And art made tongue-tied by authority.

An honest man,
close-buttoned to the chin.

- William Cowper

The jaws of darkness do
devour it up.

- Shakespeare

The Chin and Jaw

The chin and jaw symbolize aspects of will, the capacity that allows us the freedom to choose, another uniquely human characteristic—and arguably the most important one.

The chin is the forward point, the prominence, of the lower jaw. Some researchers theorize that chins may have evolved to give man a more fierce and aggressive aspect in the face of adversity. This theory fits well with colloquialisms that symbolize the relationship between the chin and aggression. Thus, a well-developed chin suggests strength in adversity, and an underdeveloped chin suggests weakness in adversity.

The ability to "take it on the chin" suggests that a person is able to endure. Thrusting out the chin, then, as a form of defiance or invitation to combat is body language that is easily understood. "Keep your chin up" encourages an individual's efforts to be courageous and persistent. Conversely, other expressions suggest victimization, such as "taking it on the chin," "leading with his chin," or "sticking his chin out," as if inviting a punch.

Ho,
the pretty page,
with...
dimpled chin
That has never
known
the barber's shear.

- Thackery

Hair on a man's chin perhaps adds to the suggestion of (primitive) aggression (a quality more associated with the male)—the defiance toward the wolf voiced by the three little pigs is inflated by references to the hair on their combative chinny chin chins. Lack of hair on the chin is the mark of youth and innocence, perhaps even vulnerability, as the skin is exposed, while beards and moustaches seem to reflect an individual's entrance into the world of adult males, signifying virility and a tradition of dominance. Beards have historically and variously indicated social status, religious position, and authority.

Another line of research suggests that the development of the chin in humans appears to parallel the development of the capacity for speech. Humans are the only animals with chins—not even our close cousins, the higher apes, have chins. Thus, evolution of a chin preordained speech, evolution of a larger brain, enhanced mental activities, and free(er) will, i.e., the ability to choose, to move beyond instinctual drives. Rodin's sculpture *The Thinker* showcases the mental aspects related to the chin; the position of the hand to the chin and body position overall creates an impression of indecision, inability to choose—likely a projection of Rodin's view of life at that time.

One of the most dramatic developments in the appearance of the human face throughout its long ancestral history is that of the size and shape of the jaw. It is likely that the change in diet from strictly vegetarian to meat eating, the advent of tools with which to process and eat food and, even more so, cooking food, diminished the need for powerful jaw muscles and large teeth for grinding. Little Red Riding Hood's surprised comment to the disguised wolf, "My, what big jaws you have," could as well have been directed to our ancestors hundreds of thousands of years ago. In modern times, some variation in jaw size provides a framework to produce faces that are square, round, or more ovoid. As a general rule, regardless of any genetic variations in races or localities, women have smaller jaws while men's are heavier.

We easily picture jaws "locking onto" something, as in the jaws of a steel trap which will hold until pried apart to release its catch, or the jaws of a bulldog equally determined to hold on indefinitely. A rigid individual is referred to as "tight jawed," and someone may "set his jaw" on a course of action. Another person, unable to act, is "slack-jawed." Thus, the jaw symbolizes determination, tenacity, and aggression— or lack thereof.

Beware the Jabborwock, my son the jaws that bite.

- Lewis Carroll

The reduction in size of the jaw and the development of the chin, as well as the evolution of a larger and more capacious forehead to accommodate changes in brain size and shape, were the principal modifications ultimately giving the face its distinctive human appearance. These changes combined with the development of the opposable thumb allowing humans to grasp, literally and figuratively, and the associated process toward lateralization of the brain formed a "package deal" rather than a random assortment of modifications of separate features. The development of the chin and the capacity for speech, along with the development of brain hemisphere specialization, meant that we humans had increasing choices to make as well as an increasing capacity to make and communicate these choices.

It appears that decision-making, i.e., employing the will to make a choice, and the amount of determination behind the choice made—including following through with the decision—are uniquely symbolized in and by the chin and jaw. Hence, Kinoetic responses that call attention to these areas are particularly important.

General Attributes

*I am
the doubter
and the doubt.*

- Emerson

The chin indicates and symbolizes a person's power to choose—that is, free will. While the conflict may be related to a perception that someone or something has power over a person, it is ultimately a conflict about whether the person can recognize that the power lies within himself. Conflicts significant enough to create uncertainty or doubt that interfere with making a decision, i.e., with choice, are symbolized by touching the chin.

The chin has two highly significant points, one at either side (overlying the bony prominences known as mental tuberosities), which are associated with both power and authority. Rubbing them simultaneously in a stroking manner is classically symbolic of wondering. It is interesting to speculate about "wonder," which is ultimately about the unknown—or beyond what can be (directly) known—and also about why these points are the ones that need stimulation when wondering. Perhaps it relates to ultimate wonder, the mystery unfolding, and whether to submit or commit one's will, i.e., "willing" versus "willful" ("not willing").

Touching the jaw refers to conflict about or problems with issues about determination—too much, too little—or issues that undermine determination. It may also refer to "reverse" determination, i.e., stubbornness. Usually these issues manifest as neurotically driven behavior or, conversely, as inability to commit to or complete things. The movement of the jaw either forward or backward, causing the chin to thrust forward or retract, indicates an individual's attitude in regard to following through on a decision, that is, whether to advance or retreat—reflecting either approach or avoidance.

It isn't really Anywhere! It's somewhere else Instead!

- A.A. Milne

Illustrations

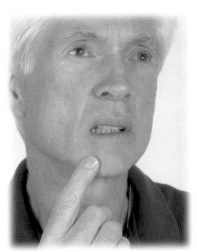

1.
A finger to the side of the chin on the lateral aspect usually is associated with issues of *power and authority*—most importantly, one's inner sense of having power in choice or in choosing. A person who frequently touches this point often seems to have underlying issues or unresolved conflicts relating to ultimate power and authority, i.e., a parent or God, or God as parent, or parent as God.

Not what we have, but what we use; Not what we see, but what we choose.

- Clarence Urmy

2.
When both points of the chin are touched, it is often done in a stroking manner and then is interpreted as *wondering*. It might better be thought of as an attempt to stimulate the mental "power points." Wonder is a response to the unknown, particularly the powerful unknown, which for many is God.

3.
Stroking here may progress to pinching the chin, which seems to be a *movement beyond wondering* by "pulling the opposites together," as if attempting to coax the specific from the general, the known from the unknown.

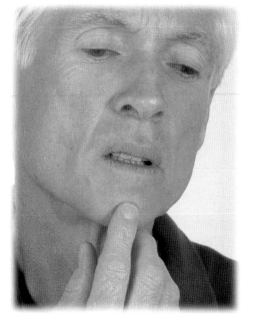

4.
When the finger is placed in the center of the chin in a stationary manner or, even more so, when the chin is stroked downward it seems to indicate *doubting or uncertainty*.

Your doubts are the private detectives Employed by your dislike, to make a case Against change or choice.

- W.R. Rodgers

5.
The finger may be stationary or may move with a side to side motion along the crease of the chin, indicating *a block to making a decision*, i.e., how to exercise will. It seems as if one is *placing doubt* in the way of letting one's truth come through.

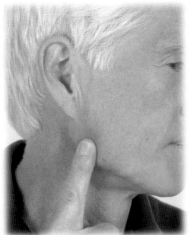

6.
The finger on the corner of the jaw suggests an issue with *determination*, as overly determined, or determined in spite of (the consequences), or as the highest priority (without regard to balance). It also refers to conflict *impairing consistent determination.*

7.
The finger behind the corner of the jaw indicates conflict concerning what is *behind a person's determination*, i.e., something driving the individual, likely impairing his freedom of choice.

8.
When the finger is inserted between the mandible and the mastoid (between the corner of the jaw and the bony prominence behind it), the reference is to *an obstacle to determination or tenacity.*

9.
A finger under the jaw indicates something (e.g., one's attitude or belief) that refers to *difficulty determining* what is important.

So long as a man imagines that he cannot do this or that, so long is he determined not to do it... it is impossible to him that he should do it.

- Benedict Spinoza

10.

The fingers under the jaw suggest *inability to speak*, to open one's mouth fully, as though blocked. The obstacle may be either external pressure or a person's own internal conflict.

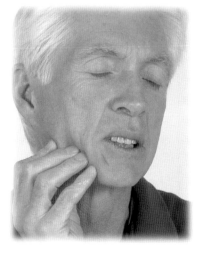

11.
Fingers along the jaw itself suggest that one is *locked into something*. This is a particularly important sign as it suggests the issue, item, theme, or belief will be very difficult to change.

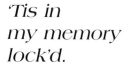

'Tis in my memory lock'd.

- Shakespeare

12.
The protruding jaw is *challenging*, as a challenge to battle. It may be underscored by a person's emphasizing hand, indicating an *internal push* toward battle.

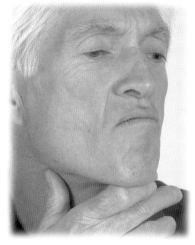

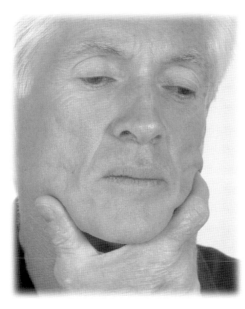

*Though a man
be wise,
It is no shame
for him
to live and learn.*

- Sophocles

13.
Fingers placed on the underside of the jaw, framing it or holding it, seems to indicate that one is *attempting to maintain face,* as though working against shame, which would bring a person down.

14.
When the framing is higher, with the fingers framing the bottom of the face or jaw, the reference seems to be that one is *evaluating*, perhaps *feeling wise* and then often with *arrogance.*

*Falls not the axe upon
the humbled neck.*

- Shakespeare

*Resolved to take Fate
by the throat.*

- Louisa May Alcott

The Neck and Throat

The extraordinary flexibility of the neck, having seven cervical vertebrae assigned to it alone, makes it possible for the head to move in various directions and maintain various positions. This ability, or lack of it, to look around and take in what is happening elsewhere is the inherent symbolism indicated by touching the neck. Conflicts manifesting in the neck refer to or concern the degree of flexibility within an individual, that is, the ability to take in other points of view or see other possibilities, or not.

As the design of the neck is to allow maximum movement of the head, emotions associated with restriction of the neck will primarily be felt as frustration or as "a pain in the neck," referring usually to an external source of difficulty but also to one's own inherent limitations in being flexible and adaptable.

And Jehovah went on to say to Moses: "I have looked at this people and here it is a stiff-necked people."

- The Bible: Exodus

"Stiff necked" suggests an inability to be flexible, out of arrogance, vanity, or haughtiness. "Rubber neck" indicates excessive curiosity or nosiness, suggesting that a person is overly interested in what others are doing.

When a person goes to an extreme in order to accomplish something, he may be said to be "breaking his neck," or when taking a risk he is "sticking his neck out." By contrast, "saving his neck" indicates a survival instinct or perhaps simply selfishness. We express feeling coerced when an individual is "breathing down our necks," and speak of punishment as "getting it in the neck."

The throat, as the specific part of the neck extending from the chin to the notch between the collarbones, has a strong emotional component. The possibility of sudden death is closely associated with the throat because it is a particularly vulnerable part of the body due to its relative exposure and the elements it contains. Carnivores go for the throat to defeat a competitor or slay their prey. We experience an imminent fear of death when we are choking, whether due to an obstruction of the airway by food or a foreign object, or constriction by an external force. Reference to the throat's vulnerability to attack is expressed by the phrases "flew at his throat," and "jumped down his throat." When someone is said to have "cut his own throat," the reference is to self-sabotage, self-defeat.

A person who is "choked up" is too emotional to speak, and words that are hard to say become "stuck in my throat." This reference may also be applied if someone's actions are unacceptable as: "His refusal to help just sticks in my throat," like a bone lodged there. Similarly, a falsehood heard may be "hard to swallow."

General Attributes

The neck moves and positions the head. Thus, touching the neck anywhere could indicate problems with restriction of movement, such as inflexibility, rigidity, or unwillingness to look at or face a source of conflict. It seems that these motions are even more symbolic in respect to touching the sides of the neck.

The hand to the back of the neck more often refers to felt responsibility, which may be associated with and symbolized by feeling "weighed down" or "burdened." Touching the back of the neck may also indicate a "pain in the neck," as if hit on the neck or dealt a blow from behind.

Fear death?—
to feel the fog
in my throat.

- Robert Browning

I feel a sort of
yearnin' 'nd
a chokin'
in my throat.

- Eugene Field

The neck/throat is the juncture between the head and body and thus has both mental and emotional components and symbolism. The uppermost part of the neck/throat is associated with a sense of vulnerability and, when excessive, may restrict or block expression as it represents a potential attack or produces the feeling of being choked, including "choked up."

I do not know why this confronts me, This sadness, this echo of pain.

- Heinrich Heine

The lower neck/throat may be the site of disrupted energy due to unresolved conflict resulting in mood swings. It is also associated with overstimulation and understimulation; in either case, a person feeling repressed in turn produces thinking that is confused or biased, resulting in a vicious cycle. In reference to confused thinking, the hand is often placed at the base of the neck covering the thyroid gland.

Illustrations

1.

One or more fingers touching or stroking the muscular cord of the right anterior neck muscle, which functions to turn the head in the opposite direction (the sternocleido-mastoid), seems to indicate the *position of one side of the body toward the opposite side*—in this example, the right (male) side toward the left (female) side. The right side (left brain) is indicating conflict in regard to the left side (the right brain's feeling state, values, etc.).

2.
Pulling on the skin of the throat, one seems to be *trying to bring oneself to say something.*

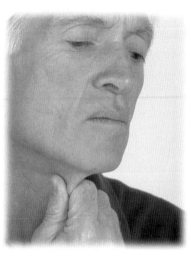

3.
Holding the throat may be done in such a way as to indicate that one is *feeling choked* or that something is *stuck* in one's throat. It may also mean *choked up,* finding it *difficult to speak.*

I had the most need of blessing, and "Amen" Stuck in my throat.

- Shakespeare

4.
The hand stroking closer to the base of the neck often indicates *a problem with mood.* It is sometimes associated with feelings of *giving up,* accompanied by *confused thinking and repression* (e.g., of a significant emotional trauma), and consequent problems with energy. (See thyroid in Body.)

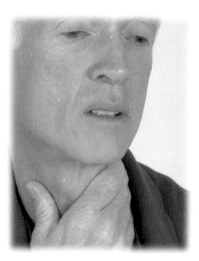

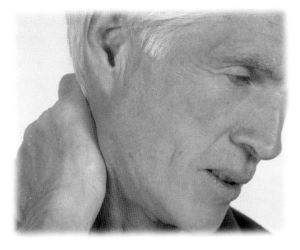

5.
A hand to the back of the neck seems to indicate that the subject matter is causing *a pain in the neck*, literally or figuratively. It often relates to *a sense of betrayal*; while a person may perceive apparent betrayal by others, it is frequently a conflict about betraying or having betrayed oneself. The head is usually tilted simultaneously with this motion. Chronic stress and tension of these posterior muscles often do produce a felt pain.

We are betrayed by what is false within us.

- George Meredith

6.
Holding the strap muscles on the side of the neck indicates that one is being held in such a way as to *not be able to look to that side*, as if restrained by the opposite side.

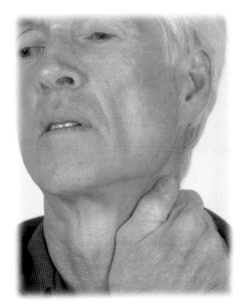

7.

The hands around the neck may be positioned in such a way as to suggest a *noose* around the neck, or that one is being *held back or held in position* by someone or something, which may be either internal or external.

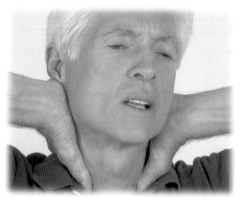

8.

One hand on the trapezius indicates conflict about *responsibility* or a sense of being *burdened*. Both hands on the trapezius, as illustrated, usually refers to a sense of *doubly burdened or weighed down*, as by a millstone.

It were better for him that a millstone were hanged about his neck, and he cast into the sea.

- The Bible: Luke

9.

Two hands behind the neck pulling downward suggest feeling constrained, even *yoked*. This also may relate to a sense of *both sides feeling betrayed*.

*Ah, what is more blessed
than to put cares away,
when the mind lays by its burden.*

\- Catullus

Put your shoulder to the wheel.

\- Aesop

*The sentiments embodied in the
Declaration of Independence
gave promise that in due time
the weights would be lifted
from the shoulders of all men.*

\- Abraham Lincoln

The Shoulder

The shoulder is the hinge for the entire arm which cannot be raised without its healthy involvement. The "frozen shoulder" syndrome makes the arm quite useless.

The relative widths of shoulders and hips are features of the body that help to distinguish gender, and the generally broader, stronger shoulders of the male might be expected to carry more of the load. Hunting—historically a male activity—required first the use of a spear or bow and subsequently the rifle, and the shoulders carried these weapons as well as game at the end of the hunt. Thus, it seems the shoulder and its implied strength is somewhat more symbolic of the male, as hips are more symbolic of the female.

Hence, expressions such as "shoulder to shoulder," "shoulder to the wheel," and "shouldering the load" seem more male oriented or at least refer to more masculine activities. Throughout history, males have been asked to volunteer for difficult missions, and we think of raising the arm as an indication of "I will (go)."

Today, the roads all runners come. Shoulder-high, we bring you home.

- A.E. Housman

The image of strength carries over into such expressions as "shoulder high," which may suggest victory, as a winning coach is lifted onto the shoulders of his players—or death, as one may be carried in a casket at that level. We "stand on the shoulders" of those who have gone before us, particularly those who have done great things. The supportive shoulder is offered for comfort or protection and is a "shoulder to cry on," but a person who is turned away receives a "cold shoulder."

General Attributes

*Touching the shoulder references the **application** of will. It seems to indicate a sense of a wrong use of will—that is, wrongdoing whether by omission or commission, and thus is associated with guilt. It seems a person signifies guilt by touching the shoulder as if "shouldering the burden" of wrongdoing, most often one's own but also sometimes that of another.*

*Conflicts regarding **availability** of will, rather than its misuse, are also signified by touching the principal muscle moving the shoulder joint, the deltoid.*

Illustrations

1.

A hand to the shoulder often signifies that one is feeling *guilt* about something yet unaddressed, something omitted or committed. It is easy to think of metaphors relating to shoulder, such as "shouldering" the burden, blame, etc.

2.

The hand placed on the shoulder so that it covers an additional area of the lung field conveys not only *guilt* but associated *sadness, grief, or longing.* (See lung field in Body.)

Secret guilt by silence is betrayed.

- John Dryden

For grief is proud, And makes his owner stoop.

- Shakespeare

3.
Touching further down the arm on the deltoid (the muscle that raises the arm to signify "I will" or to volunteer), usually refers to an *unwillingness to do or participate, or disclose*—as in an act of uncovering. Touching the back of the deltoid also signifies unwillingness but in the sense of *holding something back*—as if the arm were extended backward to withhold, restrain, or protect.

But now that ye're down we'll not turn a cold shoulder to ye.

- "Mr. Dooley"

4.
The fingers in this photo are touching the clavicle, the key strut of the shoulder girdle from which the arm hangs and which holds the arm in position to function. This response generally symbolizes the sense that *the side of the arm being touched* (as well as that aspect of one's self) *feels unsupported* in attempting to meet external stressors—as though the bone is broken and the support that should be there is not. (A broken collarbone virtually destroys the capacity of the arm to function.)

*Or to take arms
     against a sea of troubles.*

- Shakespeare

*In all ways he has to elbow himself
through the world,
giving and taking offence.*

- Thomas Carlyle

The Arm and Elbow

Once upright, early hominids made efficient use of the abilities of their freed-up arms, using them for reaching, lifting, holding, carrying, protecting the body. The arms enabled a greater range of defensive maneuvers such as shielding the body from attackers and offensive actions such as throwing objects. The simple act of waving the arms or hefting a large branch seemed to extend the size of the body, resulting in the appearance of a larger and more noteworthy foe.

Perhaps this is why we call weapons "arms," as they are extensions of the defensive/offensive capabilities of our extremities. Being "up in arms" indicates a readiness to take action, even indignation. If we feel helpless, our arms might hang limply and inactively at our sides.

The king's arm is very long.

- Herodotus

Arms are indicative of authority, and we speak of the "long arm of the law." We recognize authority with a formal salute. The wave of a hand is a casual salute in recognizing a friend, an equal.

We embrace and hug with the arms; they reach out, support—we greet a loved one with "open arms." If we wish to have little to do with someone, however, we keep that person at "arm's length."

The joints of the arm—elbow and wrist—provide remarkable flexibility and versatility to the arm. While the wrist is the more flexible and provides the most versatility in movements of the hand, an impairment of the elbow has greater impact on the usefulness of the arm. The elbow joint allows us to bring food to our mouths, cradling comfort to infants, and gives thrust to a warrior's sword. The versatility of the elbow is also suggested by referring to doing strenuous work as using "a lot of elbow grease."

The elbow often refers to a sense of combativeness and the quest for personal space. A person might "elbow" his way through a crowd until he finds "elbow room." The hard bony point of the elbow is potentially an effective weapon and, at the very least, a poke with the elbow is sure to get someone's attention.

Some expressions with reference to arms and elbows suggest closeness or nearness, as when people are "arm in arm," "elbow to elbow," or "rubbing elbows."

Our horizon is never quite at our elbows.

- Thoreau

A common position of the arms folded across the body, as shown in this photo, is often interpreted as a sign of defensiveness. Generally this is not an intentional gesture, however, but rather a Kinoetic response to the *perception of a personal attack* and the conflict that engenders.

When it is a gesture, the position of the folded arms in front of the body, higher up and slightly away from the chest, can be interpreted as if to say, "Oh yeah?" Perhaps that position amounts to an effort to enlarge one's space and bulk and thus can be seen as more aggressive than defensive. (Over fifteen meanings have been ascribed to this position!)

As a Kinoetic response, the hands and arms are brought to the body to cover the vital midsection where many emotions are strongly felt. Most people assuming this position are not aware of the complex of emotions being experienced at that moment. With increased attention to our bodies and the circumstances under which we react with this movement, most of us will become aware that we are responding to feelings in one or more of the organs and glands that underlie the folded arms. (See Body for the complex of emotions.)

This position is also assumed when a person feels a need for comfort, as a wish to be hugged. In such an instance it has been described as a *self-intimacy,* as noted in Chapter 2, and is distinguishable from both a Kinoetic response and a gesture by the context and duration of the position.

General Attributes

Respect a man, he will do the more.

- James Howell

The symbolism as expressed in our personal body language always relates to the structure of the body and the function of that part. The symbolism seems even more specific in the musculature of the limbs than other parts of the body, as each muscle has a well-defined action. The functions of the arm muscles—be they to lift, hold, carry, protect, or defend—all seem readily indicated in our Kinoetic responses.

The elbow joint and the knee joint are similar in that touching them signals issues relating to respect, authority, and superiority. They seem to differ, however, in that the elbow tends to indicate issues relating to the person himself—that is, his use of his own authority and its effect (good or ill) on others or on himself, including his self-respect; whereas the knee seems to refer to areas of conflict external to the individual.

Illustrations

1.
A hand to the biceps often refers to *uncertainty* or conflict about *the ability to provide or protect or carry the load*, or conflict about *taking action or not taking action*, perhaps on someone's behalf.

Every man shall bear his own burden.

- The Bible: Corinthians

2.
When the unprotected bony spot on the side of the arm is touched and localized quite precisely (humerus), it suggests that someone is *feeling exposed or vulnerable* to being easily hurt.

'Tis cruelty To load a fallen man.

- Shakespeare

3.
The back under side of the upper arm suggests *something hidden*, as if it were secretively held behind us.

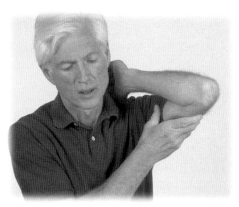

4.
The muscles of the forearm, particularly the long muscle (brachio radialis), are easily defined when the forearm is in the functional position (as when using a hammer), and touching here seems to refer to conflict about *performing or doing.*

Heaven ne'er helps the man who will not act.

- Sophocles

5.
The middle back of the forearm generally indicates a sense of conflict because of a *need to protect oneself*, as if shielding oneself, with associated *defensiveness and resistance.*

6.
The low back of the forearm generally indicates *dismissal.*

The other side of the forearm, anterior side, seems to refer to *oppositionality, protest, or refusal.* Both the anterior forearm and the posterior forearm at times have been identified with *rebelliousness and protest.*

7.
The back of the upper aspect of the elbow indicates a *resistance* (as in being dragged into something).

8.
The elbow itself seems to relate to issues of *authority and superiority*, often referring to conflict about whether to "elbow" one's way in relationship to others.

The elbowing self-conceit of youth.

- James Lowell

9.
The anterior aspect of the elbow joint (the ante-cubital fossa) seems to indicate an issue about *self-respect or self-worth*, including lack of it, which may be provoked by someone showing lack of respect.

10.
Touching the inner side of the elbow refers to an issue *in respect to oneself*. (It is the part of the elbow that comes into contact with oneself.)

Now my soul has elbow room.

- Shakespeare

In one hand he is carrying a stone,
while he shows the bread in the other.

\- Plautus

The Hand and Wrist

Other than our facial expression, the use of our hands is the next most common form of body language. Using our hands we gesture to others, literally give and take, support and touch. We display anger or aggression with a clenched fist or a striking hand. Just as hands are highly visible when used in performance of gestures to communicate with others, they are also important signals in Kinoetic responses. We demonstrate personal conflictual matters with motions of the hand or hands to the body, and also by the position of one hand relative to the other hand.

This relative positioning of the hands strongly conveys a sense of how the brain hemispheres are interacting—cooperatively or competitively—at any given moment. When the hands move in unison, in the same direction, the motion suggests that our brains might be working toward an integrated whole. The presentation of two opposing views, however, may be indicated by the divergence of hand positioning, sometimes to the extreme of pointing in the opposite direction ("on the one hand…but on the other"). Among the most interesting signals are those occurring when the hands are partially joined but at the same time indicate opposition—as when the fingers are intertwined but the thumbs are firmly pushing against each other. In extreme responses, a color change can be noted in the hands because of the pressure of one hand or finger on another.

Hands are also important tools of our interpersonal communication, as in the myriad readily understood gestures used in all cultures and societies. Shaking hands is seen as a display of friendship or welcome, but it may have originated as a way to keep the hands in the open to show that nothing dangerous was being hidden, such as a weapon.

There is a prohibition… That cravens my weak hand.

- Shakespeare

The symbolism of the hand as transactional and representing a multitude of behaviors is conveyed in expressions that portray varied relationships. Union is expressed as "hand in hand," usefulness as being "handy"; "having to hand it to" someone is complimentary, whereas a child who is difficult to control is a "handful." Significant limitations of any kind are referred to as "handicaps," and people living at a subsistence level are living "hand to mouth."

If something is placed "in our hands," it indicates our responsibility for it, whereas "out of our hands" suggests something out of our control. When we are unable to act, "our hands are tied," and then perhaps we "throw up our hands" in exasperation. Participation is implied when we "have a hand" in a situation; however when we "sit on our hands," we take no part. A "heavy hand" is oppressive, and someone who is "high handed" may be seen as arrogant.

The wrist is the most complex joint in the body and the seven carpal bones that comprise the wrist joint allow an extraordinary variety of positions. The symbolism of the wrist is largely around flexibility, be it excessive flexibility or inflexibility. For the hand itself to be strong, the wrist must be held in a slightly extended (flexed backward) and fixed position. Thus, a person who is referred to as "limp-wristed" is generally perceived as weak. The wrist is often adorned by bracelets or watches, ornamentation that tends to call extra attention to the position and activity of the hands. Another singular characteristic of the wrist is that it is easily grabbed so that a person may be forcefully restrained, most dramatically with the use of handcuffs (perhaps better referred to as wristcuffs).

Lay thou thy soul full in her hands.

- John Ruskin

The imposition of a mightier hand.

- Lord McCauley

The pulse is usually taken at the wrist where it is superficial and convenient—although it can be taken at many places on the body where the arteries can be palpated—thus, the pulse is commonly associated with the wrist. For millennia the Chinese in particular have used pulse taking at the wrist as a primary diagnostic tool. Since the pulse is an indicator of overall health and energy, it is no wonder we use the phrase "pulse of life." As the pulse has a recurrent and rhythmic beat, such an expression as "pulse of the city" connotes the energy or vibration of city life.

A pulse in the eternal mind, no less.

- Rupert Brooke

Evidence in hominid history strongly supports the coincidental developmental leap in the evolution of both the human brain and the hand. Our hand is distinguished by the oppositionality of the thumb which dramatically increases the hand's versatility and efficiency. If the thumb did not oppose the fingers, we could not "grasp" (a word that has both literal and metaphorical implications serving to describe activities of the hand and the brain). The symbolism of the thumb, then, is highly significant and indicates a desire to get control of or maintain a grasp on a person or situation. An individual may want to keep someone "under his thumb," or indicate a defiant reaction to attempts to be controlled by "thumbing his nose." Giving "thumbs down" is a clear sign of disapproval, or worse.

You yourself Are much condemn'd to have an itching palm.

- Shakespeare

In addition to the symbolism of the thumb, the other parts of the hand hold particular references as well. The palm of the hand has always been suggestive of stealth or secretiveness. To "palm" something implies stealing; the term "itchy palm" is often associated with greed. And we dispose of something unwanted by "palming it off."

Fingers have symbolism both individually and collectively. We may "finger" someone who is guilty, put a "finger on" an exact memory, miss an opportunity that has "slipped through our fingers," and "keep our fingers crossed" for another chance. A person who makes no effort to help does not "lift a finger."

General Attributes

The hand is used for, and hence symbolizes, holding, supporting, guiding, restraining. One's hand may do these things not only toward another person but toward oneself, including toward one's other hand. The interaction between the two hands reflects the interaction between our right and left brain hemispheres.

The palm is about holding and receiving; an itchy palm, both metaphorically and physically, seems to symbolize wanting to be given something.

All fingers are pointers, not just the index finger. The middle finger points usually in obscene ways, the ring finger points to commitment, and the little finger indicates "little by contrast" and occasionally evil. (Having been told as a child that one should "never point"—meaning with the index finger—the middle finger might replace the index finger as the primary pointer, but with no intent to indicate obscenity.)

The issues of conflict around the thumb are usually about the legitimacy and motives for our wish to be oppositional or domineering.

Touching the back of the wrist seems to concern flexibility, whereas ouching the front often seems to be about life—"the pulse of life."

They shall bear thee upon their hands, lest thou dash thy foot against a stone.

- The Bible: Psalms

Illustrations

Give me your hand and let me feel your pulse.

- Shakespeare

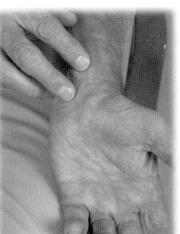

1.
Scratching the pulse at the **front** of the wrist seems to indicate something blocking one's *life energy*, as the pulse has historically signified the degree of one's vitality.

2.
Scratching, touching, rubbing the **back** of the wrist refers to being *blocked* from being able to manage/handle something, indicating inflexibility.

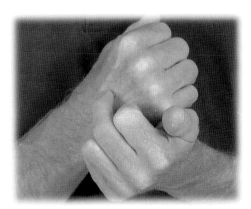

3.
Scratching the back of the hand suggests *resistance* to someone or something, perhaps to love; or there may be *diminished energy* available to deal with an issue due to resistance. It may also refer to an *insult* and "getting back at."

4.
You cannot shake hands with a clenched fist.
- Indira Gandhi

In relationship to each other, the hands support, restrain, override, or point out something about the other side. The positioning of the hands manifests most clearly the manner and degree to which the brain hemispheres are relating at that moment.

5.
Placing one hand into the other seems to refer directly to the *male/female relationship*, one side placing itself in the care of the other side, asking for support.

6.
One hand on top of the other indicates one side *dominating* the other, restraining, holding the other side down.

As a harper lays his open palm Upon his harp to deaden its vibrations.

- Longfellow

*The change
has come, she's
under my
thumb.*

- The Rolling Stones

*He read each
wound, each
weakness clear—
And stuck
his finger on
the place
and said—
Thou ailest here,
and here.*

- Thomas Hardy

7.
Scratching the thumb may indicate *oppositionality*. Touching at the base of the thumb (thenar eminence) may refer to *paralyzing the oppositional* (affecting a person's ability to be in opposition to). Touching the pad of the thumb may refer to a wish to keep *someone else under one's thumb*.

8.
When a finger
reaches the
back of the hand in the spot indicated, it seems to indicate *resistance*, specifically to certain emotions that relate to that spot (small intestine meridian), including feelings of *vulnerability, being lost, abandoned, rejected, or deserted*.

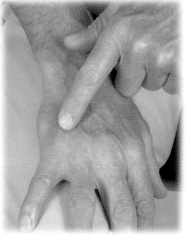

9.
Scratching the forefinger is clearly an unconscious attempt to *point to something or point something out*, and is usually quite an important sign. It is primarily an aid to bring to the conscious level something that is being overlooked.

He smote them hip and thigh.

- The Bible: Judges

The Hip

The hips are more prominent in females due to the wider pelvis, which allows for childbirth, and are as distinctive a feature to women as shoulders are to men. As a woman's hips are more mobile than a man's, and since this mobility is enhanced by activity, be it walking, dancing, etc., it markedly contributes to sex appeal. When carrying a child, mothers often put the child on the hip where the arm is easily employed for support. The top of the hip carries most the weight of the child, allowing flexibility for the mother and the comfort of a natural rocking motion for the child.

The hip joint, the largest in the body, is the hinge for and the attachment of the legs to the body. The hip joint itself is several inches down from what we commonly refer to as the hips and, since it is deeper within the body, it is the only major joint in the body that is relatively inaccessible to the touch. When someone puts her "hands on her hips," she is really putting them on the top rim of the pelvic bone.

He would not budge an inch.

- Cervantes

This hip joint determines the position of the entire body, whether standing, sitting, crouching, squatting, or curled up in a ball. The physical position a person assumes correlates with the position of her hip joint, and often reflects the position the person is taking toward a specific issue or aspects of her life. For example, a person who feels "unable to stand up to" to a challenge may signal this (frozen) position by touching the area over the hip joint.

The hip position is an important factor in producing a "stance" that a person takes as, for example, when standing with both hands firmly on the hips with the legs apart, indicating an aggressive or intimidating mode. In another typical stance, the obvious position of one hip thrust out to the side and the hand placed on the hip suggests impatience or even disgust. These stances are often Kinoetic responses but may be understood as gestures if the position is intended for communication with another person. (The symbolism of the hands on the hips with its associated emotions is discussed in the section on Body.)

To have someone "on the hip" is an ancient term meaning someone is at a disadvantage, likely relating to the incapacitation that would occur if an opponent were seriously injured on the hip.

If I catch him once upon the hip, I will feed fat the ancient grudge I bear him.

- Shakespeare

General Attributes

The hand over the hip joint refers to the position one has taken, or the position in which one has been placed by others.

Illustration

1.
When the hand is specifically over the hip joint, the reference is to the *position one has taken*, as anatomically the hip determines the standing, sitting, or recumbent position.

*A man should be upright,
not be kept upright.*

- Marcus Aurelius

If ye would go up high,
then use your own legs!

\- Nietzsche

The Leg

Our legs give us support, balance, and mobility, and their versatility is shown not only in our ability to walk and run, but to swim, operate a bicycle, dance, hop, etc. Legs enable us to approach or avoid and even move sideways as an interim solution; but our legs may also put us into precarious situations such as tripping on a curb, stepping on ice. Ambivalence is expressed in the phrase "straddling a fence," with a leg on each side.

As long as a man stands in his own way, everything seems to be in his way.

- Emerson

A person "takes a stand" in announcing his position about something; conversely, he may feel blocked when things "stand in his way" and, worse, may even "stand in his own way." We may speak of standing on solid ground, but it is more a matter of how solid our legs are on that ground. If we lack a basis for our position or argument, we "don't have a leg to stand on." And having reached a state of exhaustion or having run out of options, we may be "on our last legs."

Legs indicate action taken and power asserted; we help a person advance or succeed by "giving him a leg up," yet we may also trick and deceive by "pulling his leg."

She saw two legs were lost on him Who never meant to run.

- George Canning

General Attributes

Touching the leg carries the same kind of symbolic information as touching the arm in that the symbolism relates quite specifically to the anatomical and functional aspects of the muscles and their well-defined action. Touching the leg may indicate conflict about moving toward or away from, or problems with stepping aside or moving laterally. It may relate to the ability to carry on or carry a burden, or stand up to, stand on one's own, etc.

The groin and upper thigh have sexual symbolism, likely because of the proximity to the genital area. Touching the back of the thigh refers to feeling reduced or made little, as belittled, by a person or a situation.

The lower leg is about maintaining one's position, standing or holding one's ground.

*Stand
And do the best,
my lad.*

- A.E. Housman

Upper leg

Illustrations

1.

The groin not surprisingly relates to passion, that is, libido, which includes but probably is not exclusively sexual energy. A hand placed on the groin signifies *a block to one's passion.*

2.

The **front** of the thigh relates to sexuality. A stationary hand may refer to a *block to sexuality, hesitancy or resistance*; rubbing the thighs indicates (unexpressed) *sexual desire*, either due to a lack of awareness of the desire or because it is prohibited/forbidden.

3.

When the **lateral** thigh is touched or stroked from mid-thigh toward the knee, the motion refers to *change is difficult.* Touching the **back** of the thigh may refer to *not able to do* something, *not able to carry on*— by being made to *feel little, or by the weight of a burden*, particularly one laden with heavy emotion, as grief or excessive responsibility.

Lower leg

4.
Touching the outside of the leg seems to indicate a conflict in relation to *the issue being considered*. Touching lower down on the side of the leg, on the peroneal muscles, seems to reflect a *wish to get away from*.

5.
The posterior calf seems to refer to *the stand one takes*; conversely it may indicate *not being able to stand on one's own*. It may also less commonly refer to the stand that someone else takes.

6.
Touching the muscles of the front of the leg, as rubbing the shins, indicates that one is attempting to *hold one's ground*. The hands would have started higher and stroked down and up again.

7.
A leg drawn up to the body indicates that one side is *needing comforting*, a position common in children and in some women. The response may also indicate feeling young, *unable to stand up for oneself*. The initial stimulus for this motion is usually a sense of conflict about needing comfort and thus is a Kinoetic response. (If the position is protracted, however, it may be better described as self-intimacy—that is, settling for providing one's own comfort.)

*They fell upon their knees
and blessed the God of Heaven.*

- William Bradford

The Knee

As the elbow and wrist joints provide flexibility and versatility to the arm, so the knee and ankle joints do the same for the leg; their functions and symbolism are analogous though different. The ankle, like the wrist, is the more flexible and provides versatility in the movements of the foot. However, an impairment of the knee has a greater impact on the usefulness of the entire leg.

Don't let your sorrow come higher than your knees.

- Swedish proverb

We flex at the knee to propel us upward or forward. The knee allows us to stride, run, dance, crouch, jump. Referring to external forces that prevent us from advancing or retreating, we say we have been "cut off at the knees." If we are thoughtless in our actions we can get "knee deep" in trouble, again suggesting inability to move, as though mired in quicksand.

Frequent reference to the knee in self-touching signals that the knee is symbolic of authority. One bends the knee—genuflects—to a king or queen, and to God. If forced into this attitude of submission, we have been "brought to our knees." A "knee-jerk reaction" happens relexively in response to an external stimulus or situation.

Whereas the elbow more often suggests being one's own authority—making "elbow room" for oneself—the knee more often refers to others in authority. These references can include conflict about deference, whether it is related to submitting to or supporting an external power or, conversely, related to not receiving support from that external authority.

General Attributes

Touching or scratching the knee indicates issues relating to external power and authority, especially problems with deference or submission to authority. It is more often toward an external authority, referring to resistance to bending the knee toward someone or something "out there telling me what to do."

Touching the inner aspect of the knee may be a reference to resistance to showing support for the authority of another.

Illustrations

1.
Touching the knee refers to a conflict about *submission*, ranging from mild (e.g., *deferring* to an opinion) to extreme, as total submission and feeling *no choice*.

2.
Touching the inside of the knee may indicate *resistance to providing support* for an external authority, or a *lack of ability to support*, perhaps because a person feels "not up to the task." (The medial ligament—MCL—is a principal support for the knee.)

As princes' palaces; they that enter there must go upon their knees.

- John Webster

*It is better to die on your feet
than to live on your knees!*

- Emiliano Zapata

Make haste, the better foot before.

- Shakespeare

The Foot and Ankle

The foot has many similarities to the hand including bone structure. Although it is not nearly as versatile as the hand, of course, the foot is granted a remarkable range of motion by the ankle joint. The seemingly simple but complex process of walking hinges on the unfettered movement of the ankle. As our agent of locomotion, the foot refers to movement from one location to another by walking, running, stepping, skipping. To go "on foot" is to travel without a conveyance; when someone has "one foot in the door," a significant step has been taken to get to a desired position or place.

We stand on and balance our bodies with our feet and refer to securing a firm position by "gaining a foothold." "Standing on one's own two feet" refers to a self-supporting position or independence.

Whereas one wants to "get off on the right foot" or put one's "best foot forward" to make a good impression, references to feet may also suggest the commission of mistakes. When a person trips or stumbles "over his own feet," he has committed a clumsy error, probably one that could have been avoided with a little more attention to the matter. That mistake may be exacerbated when he "puts his foot in his mouth" or "puts his foot in it."

At her feet
he bowed,
he fell,
he lay down.

- The Bible: Joshua

As opposed to the exalted position of the head and its associated "higher" functions, the feet, located at the lowest extreme of the body, have somewhat less noble connotations. To have someone "at one's feet" refers to domination of another person and even a sense of degradation of that person. If, however, we "sit at the feet" of a wise man, the reference is more of submission to a higher intellect or spirituality; just as "wherever MacDonald sits, there is the head of the table" (see Head), individuals of lower status sit at the "foot" of the table.

The heel tends to have negative connotations. To "take to one's heels" suggests an undignified flight. To be "under one's heel" is to be dominated and controlled by another; and a "heel" is, in old-fashioned terminology, a cad. An individual who is strongly or even stubbornly disagreeing with another may "dig in his heels" on his side of the argument.

I took to my heels as fast as I could.

- Terence

General Attributes

Conflicts symbolized by the foot refer to one's "footing," to standing on one's own feet or taking a position. It may also refer to conflicts about aggressive feelings, including standing on or even stomping on someone or something.

The ankle seems to have reference similar to that of the elbow and knee in signaling issues with authority, but relates more particularly to conflict about locus of control of authority, i.e., a conflict about how much internal power a person has to be able to deal with a powerful external authority.

Illustrations

1.
Flexing the foot at the ankle, lifting the foot, is a common and important sign indicating *protest, disagreement,* or even *digging in one's heels*, analogous to "yes, but" as might be expressed in conversation.

A circular motion of the foot seems to mean *trying to get around* the conflict and/or the authority obstacle.

Happy he who could learn the causes of all things and who put beneath his feet all fears.

- Virgil

2.
Scratching the top of the arch of the foot seems to refer to conflict about a *position one is taking or being troubled by someone else's position.*

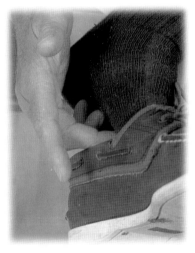

3.
Touching the bottom of the foot may indicate *trouble standing on one's own feet*. However, it may also convey the aggressive notion of *stamping on*.

4.
Touching the ankle seems to refer to an *issue with external authority*; the conflict is often around a sense of "can't go ahead" with some aspect of life until the issue is resolved. Touching the **outside** of the ankle indicates a conflict about whether to *move laterally to avoid confrontation*; touching the **inside** of the ankle suggests an inclination to *sidestep the issue* altogether.

Sudden a thought came like a
full-blown rose,
Flushing his brow,
and in his pained heart
Made purple riot.

- John Keats

The Body

When the hand is brought to the body, the motion is usually in conjunction with underlying emotion. We experience emotions throughout the body, particularly in the trunk of the body. In this section the term *body* will be interchangeable with *trunk*, that is, the body from the neck to the groin.

*When
the heart aches,
all members
partake of the
pains.*

- Cervantes

When we think thoughts or recall memories, with the associated perceptions of their significance, a *feeling complex* is created that registers in *both the body and the brain* and is accompanied by physical changes of which we may be variably aware, including those of muscle tension, pulse rate, sweating, etc. We recognize this association of physical responses, particularly to strong emotions, in our language; e.g., we "quake" with fear, "bristle" with rage. While emotional responses are innate, they are increasingly modified by life experience and one's evaluation of events.

We often experience muscle groups activated with emotion, some more than others depending on the type and intensity of the stimulus, and may be associated with an awareness of a single feeling or an admixture. An example is the contraction of the muscles around the mouth and jaws when one is confronted with a difficult challenge, associated with an identifiable *feeling* of determination. If the feeling progresses to "fierce" determination, the jaw muscles may tighten, even clench, and the lips will likely narrow. These are not invariable concomitants of the feeling of determination, as one may be aware of the feeling yet have trained oneself to modify the physiologic response.

When a residue of an emotional state and the associated feeling(s) are not resolved or released, the physiologic state persists as a chronic condition, as in repressed anger, in which there is frequently persistent tension in the head, back of the neck, and shoulders. Chronic fear may result more noticeably in tension in the lower back. These musculo-skeletal responses and the areas of sustained tension, as well as the effect on posture and gait, are studied in the field of bioenergetics.

This aspect of the expression of emotion in the musculature will not be dealt with here, nor will expression of emotion on the face. Rather, the association of emotion with organs, glands, and hollow viscera is favored in this work because of its specificity in identifying our less conscious feeling states, as well as the likelihood that unresolved conflict and the chronic emotional residue will continue to affect the associated viscera. Consequently, bringing one's attention to an area of the trunk in which a physiologic sensation is perceived can be most helpful in accessing the emotion-laden information needed to identify and help resolve the areas of conflict.

The word *feeling* is rather generic and refers to either the identifiable component of the emotional state, such as fear or joy, or may refer to the sensation of being touched by someone, or touching another person or thing. Additionally, *feel* is used by most individuals to describe a physical sensation in the body ("I feel cold") that is not obviously associated with an affect (mood). For these reasons, this term can cause considerable confusion. As referred to here, therefore, *feeling* is used to note the *affective component of an emotional state*, i.e., that which affects our state of well being positively or adversely (e.g., grief).

Designations of feeling states number in the hundreds, and attempts have been made to reduce these states, called *affective states*, to a simple scheme of origination. One concept puts it in just three dimensions,

*Distill'd
Almost to jelly
with the act of
fear.*

- Shakespeare

*But I am
pigeon-livered
and lack gall
To make
oppression
bitter.*

- Shakespeare

that of pleasantness/unpleasantness, activation/inhibition, and control/unrestraint. Another identifies a small number of basic feelings, such as fear and anger; this approach treats basic emotions as if they were primary colors on the color wheel from which all other hues are derived. One concept identifies a few fundamental attributes of many, if not all, feelings; and yet another schema involves categorizing affects as primary (innate) and secondary (acquired).

It is clear that we have basic biological drives and that they are associated with the affective response, providing motivational information concerning the time and place of response, which is the "when, where, what, to what" (Tomkins, 1962).

It is likely, although difficult to imagine, that such a complex system of emotional response has evolved from what may have been a very simple approach/avoidance mechanism among the most primitive of creatures. Stemming initially from pain and pleasure signals from the drive system, and the positive (approach) and negative (avoidance) signals from the affect (feeling) system, these simple creatures are able to conclude immediately what is acceptable or unacceptable. It is clear that we do not need to learn about the pain of hunger, the pleasure of eating, nor do we need to learn how to be afraid or to experience joy.

A simple system for catagorizing affects, both positive and negative, was devised by Silvan Tomkins who presents them along a continuum of intensity. Thus, the positive affect of interest increases to excitement, simple enjoyment increases to profound joy; the negative affect of distress increases to anguish, shame to humiliation, contempt to disgust.

A negative affect may cause the hand to be brought to the body; a positive affect will not do so as conflict is not involved. In addition to levels of intensity there are also admixtures. If a positive affect is admixed with a negative one (for example, feeling "touched" by the thanks expressed by one's child at graduation—delight in his achievement is admixed with sadness that a phase of life is over), self-referential touching may also occur.

As described in this section, the explanations of feeling states indicated by personal body language are of necessity simplified and refer to the predominant *disruptive affect* that is felt in a particular part of the body in response to conflict. This discomforting felt affect may lead a person to use the expression "I feel…," as feelings are very often described in terms of a bodily sensation; we use colloquial expressions such as "broken hearted" and "sick to my stomach" relating to where one feels something. The hand may or may not be brought to the body as the sensation is experienced; however, the hand may also be brought to the body *with no conscious experience of either sensation or the associated felt affect.*

Many people, perhaps the majority, have become largely desensitized to sensations in the body, unless they are particularly uncomfortable. Practiced awareness, however, can increasingly help an individual to recognize a change within the body before it announces itself at the level of discomfort, even if that change is hard to describe, such as feelings of heaviness or emptiness or just "different-than-usual-ness."

The emotional complex includes the release of hormones and neurotransmitters that circulate throughout the body and are "felt" in the body as a whole, that is, in cells throughout the entire body. Evidence suggests, however, that certain organs take the brunt of the emotional response, as will be discussed.

It seldom happens that any felicity comes so pure as not to be tempered and allayed by some mixture of sorrow.

- Cervantes

The Chinese Legacy

The Chinese long ago came to understand that specific patterns of emotional responses will predispose to specific organ dysfunction and, in this way, unexpressed or unreleased emotions negatively affect one's health. Classic Oriental thinking is based on the five-element theory: Emotions and the associated feelings we indentify as anger affect the *liver*, those of fear affect the *kidneys*; sadness affects the *lungs*, (the disturbance of) thinking affects the *spleen*, and (the disturbance of) joy affects the *heart*. Modern theorists in the field of Oriental medicine cannot provide an understanding of the ultimate mechanics of energy flow at this point[1] but still talk and write in metaphoric and poetic terms to describe these energy disruptions and consequences.

I am sure care's an enemy to life.

- Shakespeare

Leon Hammer writes on this topic (1991, pp. 357-376) in a manner that is more easily understood than that of many other theorists, although he, too, often relies on the more classical descriptive nosology. "An emotion," he writes, "is an energy configuration that, if it cannot be naturally and constructively expressed by the person experiencing it, will appear as excess energy in its target Organ," which will then "attempt to transform the excess energy into the particular work of that Organ." For example, on grief/sadness, he notes:

> *On the energy level we have stagnation deep inside the Lung, where the feeling and crying is hidden and blocked. [Thus] sadness involves holding back crying....The earlier and more severe the loss, the greater the effect upon Lung function on both a physical and emotional level....The physical effect of this stagnation may express itself as asthma, chronic bronchitis, recurrent upper respiratory infections, allergy, pneumonia, or even tuberculosis.*

---

[1] The thinking in Chinese medicine, as in Western medicine, continues to evolve. More recent concepts include the requirement that for the traditional theory to apply, all organs would be functioning adequately in approximate equal health.

The Chinese system is intricate and has evolved beyond the concept of an invariable correlation of one emotional state to one organ. As Hammer observes, "The phenomenon is different in sadness that originates in later life and the heart is more likely to be affected. Over the longer period of time, the liver and the kidney would more likely be involved."

When unbalancing emotions such as anger, hatred, resentment, and grief are either persistently repressed or inadequately expressed, in some way they are held in the body, restricting energy flow in proportion to the mix and intensity of emotion. Whether the restricted energy flow is produced by interference fields in areas of the body, or whether the memory is "recalled" in the body (cellular/organ memory)[2] as well as the brain, the act of spontaneously bringing the hand to the affected part of the body appears to temporarily remedy the energy defect.

The hand that is brought to the body in response to an emotion invariably covers an organ and, by doing so, can bring attention to the emotion relating to that organ. The identified emotion may be related to the experience of that moment or may prove to be related to a past event that has some associative relevance to the present event. *Aware that emotions, or some component of residual emotions, become "stuck" as a result of unresolved conflict and that the emotional impact is remembered in the body—be it in the brain, the body, or a combination—it becomes apparent that the site and action of self-referential touching allows the associated emotional complex to be recalled.*

The heartache and thousand natural shocks That flesh is heir to.

- Shakespeare

---

[2] Researchers have correlated changes in personality and preferences seen in organ transplant recipients reflecting those of the donor, which argues strongly for the concept of body or cellular memory.

The effects of disturbing emotions are most readily perceived in those areas of the organ fields represented by the shaded areas.

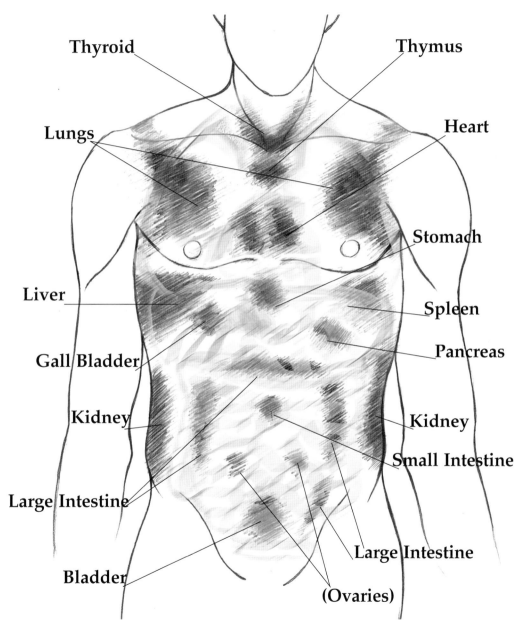

Thyroid

Thymus

Lungs

Heart

Liver

Stomach

Spleen

Gall Bladder

Pancreas

Kidney

Kidney

Small Intestine

Large Intestine

Large Intestine

Bladder

(Ovaries)

General Attributes

The photos shown in this section illustrate the types of automatic movement of the hand to the body that relate to underlying emotions and feelings, whether they are consciously acknowledged or not. In fact, it appears that the movement is more likely to occur when the emotion is not being acknowledged and the person remains in conflict concerning the matter at hand. It seems these motions—common throughout our culture and apparently throughout the world—support the ancient notion of emotions and feelings as being vested in specific parts of the body, particularly body organs and glands.

Illustrations

1.
The hand drawn to the **thyroid area** is associated with *profound hurt*, as in the perception of *not being wanted*, accompanied by *repression, confused thinking*, with consequent *mood and energy changes*.
(See Neck and Throat.)

Never give way to melancholy; resist it steadily.

- Sydney Smith

2.
A hand on the **thymus area** usually refers to feeling *deficient* in some way, being *weak and unable to defend oneself, or unable to cope*. This is closely associated with *envy*, the feeling that someone else has something one needs, without which one is deficient.

3.

The hand on the **heart** refers to some negative aspect of love such as *broken hearted, lost love, loss of a heart connection*, or the more adverse aspects of *dislike*, even *hatred*. (As with the illustration below, when done purposefully as a mode of communicating joy or sympathy, it constitutes a common gesture easily distinguishable from a Kinoetic response.)

4.

This position may indicate something *restricting one's heart*. Done with a cupped hand, it may indicate something pouring out of the **heart**, as representing *something lost*, but it could also represent the *obstacles to outpouring of love or to the desire to give love*.

Everyone can master a grief but he that has it.

- Shakespeare

5.

The hand placed on the **lung field** is a response to emotions of *sadness, grief, or longing*. It may also indicate *guilt* if localized in the upper lung area on or near the shoulder.

6.

When both hands are put under the axilla on both sides of the **lung field**, pulling upward, it seems to indicate *a longing to be supported* or even lifted up, as a child might be picked up by a parent.

7.

The hand placed on the side, underneath the axilla and still on the **lung field**, often refers to *an old longing*, often felt relative to a parent and causing conflict in reference to *one's position as son or daughter.*

Children begin by loving their parents; as they grow older they judge them; sometimes they forgive them.

- Oscar Wilde

8.

When the hand is placed further back on the **lung field**, it may indicate a *wish to get away* from someone or something.

9.
A hand to the pit of the **stomach** refers to emotions such as feeling *needy, left out, anxious about, or disgusted with.*

10.
The hand somewhat lower down on either side of the **large intestine** has more to do with the emotions often referred to as anal (perhaps more properly called "colonic"), such as *obstinacy, compulsivity, and rigidity.* (See the illustration of organ fields for other reference sites for the colon.)

An obstinate man does not hold opinions, but they hold him.

- Samuel Butler

11.
The hand covering the **liver area** usually represents *rage or anger*, or a lesser degree of anger, as *frustration.*

Individuals tend to localize the **gall bladder** (under the liver) quite specifically with the index finger. The emotion there is *resentment* or (even stronger) *galled.*

12.
When the hands are placed on the **kidneys**, the significance seems to be the feeling of *pure fear* or even *dread*.

13.
This position with the hands simultaneously on the **kidneys** and the top of the hips refers to the *wish to deal with one's fear* by taking action, facing a problem by being aggressive. This is a common position with men, but it is increasingly common with women in the competitive atmosphere of today's business world.

A man of my kidney.

- Shakespeare

14.
The important consideration in this position is that the arms and hands cover several organ fields—**kidney, liver, stomach, spleen, adrenal, colon**—and therefore may be *a response to emotions* felt in one or any combination of these areas. Individuals may say they find this posture comforting.

15.
Bringing the hand to the spleen usually references a troublesome emotion associated with a *negative self-image*, either generally or in regard to particular behavior or character flaws. The feeling is generally of *diminished self-esteem and self-love*, and is often associated with *shame*.

There is luxury in self-dispraise;
And inward self-disparagement affords
To meditative spleen a grateful feast.

— Wordsworth

Section III

Applying Kinoetics

Chapter 8

Applying Kinoetics

I begin to get a little acquainted with my own strength and weakness.

- Keats

Although this work initially was and still is largely oriented toward use in therapy, counseling, and other interpersonal work (the application of which is described later in this chapter), understanding the Kinoetic format enables people to utilize the process in other ways.

Body language concepts have generally been used to "read" others as well as ourselves–and this is also one application of Kinoetics. Imagine a situation in which an agreement seems to have been reached between two parties but even at the moment of apparently agreeing, one party is signaling conflict. Clearly, such a contract is less likely to hold up than if there were an absence of internal conflict. Thus, the party aware of the meaning of the signal might rethink the agreement. A more important example is that of individuals who are sharing deeply and intimately, during which time an opportunity may arise to cautiously frame a question based on an understnding of Kinoetics. A reminder, however: It is important to keep in mind that the thoughts and feelings provoking Kinoetic responses are private and not intended for communication. Moreover, as noted, they are most often out of the awareness of the person signaling conflict.

In specialized settings such as the classroom or the courtroom, information conveyed by Kinoetics can be significant and revealing. In the theater, seasoned actors who utilize the motions depicted here tend to do so in the appropriate context with apparently the same specificity. As far as I know, there is no textbook that teaches these motions and the inherent symbolism. Rather, the professional actor, by virtue of putting herself sufficiently in the part and experiencing the thoughts, feelings, reactions, and internal conflict of the individual being portrayed, often touches herself in the manner described here, spontaneously and without study, often producing an unaffected and natural performance.

In a different vein, we understand that transmitting personal information with body language can sometimes be disadvantageous, and one may use this knowledge to restrict one's body movement, especially self-touching. Good poker players understand the value of this type of deception. We must acknowledge that deception has value ranging from survival to managing oneself in the everyday world (where the social lie may be not only useful but even kind).

Sometimes a person in therapy will say, "I better be careful where I touch myself (lest I give away information that is private or secret)," and then appear to self-consciously restrict body motion. Most individuals, however, quickly see the irony of being deceptive in the psychotherapeutic setting, which is designed for the benefit of full disclosure in privacy and safety.

Kinoetics alerts us to our *self*-deception, the greatest obstacle on the path to self-awareness. The process of introspection required to reach this awareness is difficult as the relexes and patterns that developed in response to early life experiences often involve distressing emotions such as guilt, anxiety, shame, or grief. Thus, we resist exploring this unconscious material because of the associated pain and the affront to our persona, our self-image; understandably, the willingness to explore these areas is blocked. However with the discovery that insight can be rapid and the pain transcended, willingness to look at this material usually increases significantly; i.e., the will is "freed up" for such personal work.

Where the willingness is great, the difficulties cannot be great.

- Machiavelli

In doing psychotherapy, I have been particularly gratified to observe how a patient's understanding of Kinoetics heightens awareness of the thought/feeling complex, increasing that person's interest and willingness to explore deeper levels of consciousness. Most all patients quickly understand the symbolic significance of such movements, recognizing body signals they have taken for granted, analogous to but more specific than other body responses such as blushing, suddenly feeling warm, or becoming tense in response to thoughts or memories, and appreciate the questions they are being asked, which their own body language dictates. The questions below demonstrate what a therapist might ask.

Touching one's head or forehead can lead to a line of questioning about ideas, notions, desires, or thoughts that are waiting to break through. The query usually produces material that the person is often hesitant to express or consciously thinks isn't important, even though the facial expression shows that it is. Similarly, questions such as the following might be posed depending upon the area of the body touched: "What is it that you would be sad to see?", "Could you give me another view on that?" (see Eye); "What is it you wouldn't want to see (or hear)?" (Eye, Ear); "Is there something you had said that you wish you hadn't?", "Are there different ways of saying (something) that are competing for expression?" (Mouth); "Is there something you are unwilling to do?" (Shoulder); "Do you feel you are struggling to hold your ground?" (Leg).

If signs of disagreement within the person are noted but are not being verbalized (see Mouth), it might lead to this question: "If you were to allow yourself to disagree with what you just said—for example, starting with 'yes, but'—what would you go on to say?" This question usually

A great discovery... gives a new and clear form to what we have long been ruminating without suspecting it.

- Proust

produces a conflictual or oppositional point of view to what the individual had been saying just a moment before.

Another example would be a person rubbing her head while discussing a certain topic (see Head), indicating a difficulty with receiving guidance. When questioned about that topic, the person might indicate that it relates to the therapy itself, or to prior attempts to deal with people who are trying to influence or guide her, or even to difficulty with praying and asking for divine assistance.

Certain motions are particularly important in that they allow access to material that would otherwise be difficult to reach. Such is the case with a "terrible thought" (see Head). An example is that of an individual talking about the problem of caring for a burdensome elderly parent with whom she had experienced a poor relationship over the years. At one moment, as she touched her head, she was asked, "If you would allow a terrible thought to emerge, what would it be?" The answer was "I hate to say it, but life would be a lot easier if my mother were dead."

The response to particularly significant questions (as "what terrible thought…?") has been on countless occasions so spontaneous and apparently effortless, that *the simplicity of this approach belies its utility and effectiveness.* Experienced therapists know that material like this is slow to be acknowledged by the individual and is ultimately done so laboriously, with guilt and embarrassment—the feelings that engender the resistance to saying such things in the first place. Disclosure is readily allowed by the *timing* of the question as well as its nature, and that timing is indicated by the person herself, for *the narrow window of opportunity occurs at precisely the moment of self-touching.*

*Facing it—
always facing it—
that's the way
to get through.*

- Joseph Conrad

*Resolve to
know thyself:
and know,
that he
Who finds
himself, loses
his misery.*

- Matthew Arnold

A person familiar with Kinoetics can pose for herself the type of question that the knowledgeable therapist might ask. The pursuit of self-knowing is markedly facilitated in this way, for these areas of internal conflict and the resistance to knowing are countered at the very moment they manifest. It is unfortunate that most of us have "lost touch" with ourselves; if we concur with the ancient injunction to "know thyself," then getting back in touch with oneself is critically important.

If one is to ask, "What's troubling me?" it becomes necessary to stop and reflect a moment, seeking the nature of the inner conflict and the associated emotions. Having touched upon the problem area, the individual who understands Kinoetics is able to formulate questions based on her personal body language. Prompt recognition of conflict as it arises is essential for defining the conflict; the greater the delay, the more likely the window of opportunity will shut.

Learning to understand one's own personal body language enables disparities and contradictions to become more apparent, which is necessary before they can be resolved. Using the knowledge of Kinoetics can markedly aid the goal of resolving or at least negotiating the differences between our two brains so that one does not continually feel pulled or pushed off center. Resolution of inner conflict begins as left and right hemispheres speak in moderated debate with the goal of mutual understanding.

Going further, the *ideal* goal is that referred to by the pioneering split-brain surgeons Bogen and Vogel: the full integration of both hemispheres at all times. For most people, this can be achieved only partially and then only through rigorous mental training. Meditation orients one in this direction, as do other practices of "mindfulness."

A particularly useful sign that one has achieved this balance may be the concomitant and symmetrical use of both hands while communicating. This obviously requires the activity of the motor sections of both brain hemispheres and is usually associated with other mental activity in each hemisphere. The Dalai Lama's body language is an excellent example of this outward manifestation of mental integration, as can be observed in filmed interviews.

In applying Kinoetics, it should be noted that resolution of a conflict may not occur simply with recognition of that conflict. Rather, such a move toward understanding and awareness usually requires further thoughtful dialogue between one's opposing views and values (our two spheres of consciousness) to help us find a balance point and promote personal integration.

A caveat concering this work is that Kinoetics is only one more tool to help us develop overall awareness. Most, if not all of us, will profit from receiving assistance on this journey, whether it be from learning meditation techniques to seeking help from professionals who specialize in newer integrative therapeutic techniques.

It must be noted that preoccupation with self—narcissism—causes us to continue to obstruct the development of awareness. If we understand that we are all a "piece of the continent, a part of the main," that there is a universal energy that flows through and around us, that the unconscious is always present and always trying to manifest, then we will find ourselves moving toward greater awareness.

Cherish your emotions and never undervalue them.

- Robert Henri

*Let us not look back in anger
or forward in fear,
but around in awareness.*

\- James Thurber

References:

Becker, R. & Selden, G. (1985). *The body electric: Electromagnetism and the foundation of life.* Morrow.

Becker, R. (1990). *Cross currents.* Putnam.

Bellak, L. & Baker, S. (1980). *Reading faces.* Holt Rinehart Winston.

Birdwhistell, R.L. (1970). *Kinesics and context.* University of Pennsylvania Press.

Carus, G.C. *Psyche: On the development of the soul.* (R. Welch, Trans.) Spring Publications. (Original work published 1851.)

Damasio, A. (1994). *Descartes' error.* Avon Books.

Diamond, J. (1983). *Your body doesn't lie.* Warner Books.

Eisler, R. (1988). *The chalice and the blade.* Harper & Row.

Ekman, P. & Friesen, W. (1969). Repertoire of nonverbal behavior: categories, origins, usage, and coding. *Semiotica I.*

Ekman, P., Friesen, W. & Ellsworth, P. (1972). *Emotion in the human face.* Pergamon Press.

Ekman, P. & Friesen, W. (December, 1972). Hand movements. *The Journal of Communication.*

Ekman, P. (1992). *Telling lies.* W.W. Norton.

Galderisi, S., Mucci, A. & Maj, M. (September, 2000). Brain hemispheric organization, anxiety, and psychoses. *CNS Spectrums.*

Galin, D. (October, 1974). Implications for psychiatry of left and right cerebral specialization. *Archives of General Psychiatry.*

Gazzaniga, M. (August, 1967). The split brain in man. *Scientific American.*

Hammer, L. (1991). *Dragon rises, red bird flies: Psychology and chinese medicine.* Station Hill.

Hampden-Turner, C. (1981). *Maps of the mind.* Macmillan.

Harre, R. & Lamb, R. (1983). *The encyclopedic dictionary of psychology.*
    MIT Press.
Knapp, M.L. (1972). *Nonverbal communication in human interaction.*
    Holt, Rinehart & Winston.
Krout, M.H. (1954). An experimental attempt to determine the
    significance of unconscious manual symbolic movements.
    Journal of General Psychology.
Krout, M.H. (1954). An experimental attempt to produce unconscious
    manual symbolic movements. *Journal of General Psychology.*
Mahl, G. (1971). *Psychological conflict and defense.* Harcourt, Brace, Javanovich.
McNeill, D. (1992). *Hand and mind: What gestures reveal about thought.*
    University of Chicago Press.
Morris, D. (1977). *Manwatching.* Harry Abrams.
Ornstein, R. (1997). *The right mind: Making sense of the hemispheres.*
    Harcourt Brace.
Sagan, C. (1977). *The dragons of eden.* Ballantine.
Schwartz, G. (1996, Autumn). The ACE factor. *Noetic Sciences Review.*
Shlain, L. (1998). *The alphabet versus the goddess.* Penguin Arkana.
Sperry, R.W. (1966). Brain bisection and consciousness. J. Eccles, ed.
    Brain and conscious experience. Springer-Verlag.
Springer, S. & Deutsch, G. (1981). *Left brain, right brain.* W.H. Freeman & Co.
Tomkins, S. (1962). *Affect imagery and consciousness, Vol I.* Springer.

About the Author

William Linson received his medical degree from the National University of Ireland in 1964 and completed internship at Albany Medical Center in New York. He returned to Ireland for post-graduate training in internal medicine, and then trained in internal medicine and psychiatry at Dartmouth Hitchcock Medical Center in New Hampshire which culminated in a Fellowship in Psychosomatic Medicine. He was a Peace Corps physician in South America for two years, and a physician volunteer in Africa.

Over his career he directed psychiatric consultation services at Denver General Hospital as well as Baystate Medical Center in Massachusetts, where he became Chief of Psychiatry, and held teaching positions as Associate Clinical Professor at both Tufts University and University of Massachusetts. He has practiced psychiatry for over 30 years, and is certified with the American Board of Psychiatry and Neurology.

During the several years he was living and working in other cultures, he was struck by the fact that in spite of differences, people communicate in similar ways through facial expression and body language, an area of interest that culminated in the development of a more effective approach to therapy, as demonstrated in this work.

This work developed as part of a therapeutic approach aimed at resolving internal oppositionality, which will be covered in a forthcoming book on Integrative Therapy to be published in 2002.